Library of Congress Cataloging-In-Publication Data

ISBN 978-0-9771136-5-1

Copyright© 2008 Cynthia Vodopich. All rights reserved.

Publisher: The Old Gypsum Printer Inc./Wings Publishing
                      P.O. Box 270
                      Gypsum, CO 81637

Cover: Glenwood Springs, viewed toward the south

Cover Photography: Mark Hatch Photography and Mark and Cynthia Vodopich

Cover Design: Mark Hatch and Vincent Hidalgo

Book Design: Terri Lowery, The Old Gypsum Printer

Printer: The Old Gypsum Printer, Inc.

Printed in the United States of America

First Edition
Second Printing

April 2009

Dedication:

To Walter,
for finally letting me
write it all down
and
to all those customers that
never let me give up on this book;
pulling me aside at the grocery store,
the hardware store and razzing me at work.
Without you, this book would not
have happened.

Délice

Special Thanks:

To my husband, Mark,
whose "no excuses" attitude, financial support,
and photography and computer skills
made this book possible

To my sister, Vreni,
for all the diligent proofreading,
no matter how crazy her schedule

To Mom,
for all her trips into the basement
to get the stuff I needed,
as well as all the proofreading

To Jean,
for allowing me to be employed, sort of

To Mark Hatch Photography,
for an afternoon of patience and creativity,
and all the creative ideas

To Emma,
for helping me face my software demons

Notes

We strongly recommend that you read a recipe all the way through days before you intend to prepare it the first time. Don't just read the ingredient list. Many of these recipes happen in stages and the first stage may have to be frozen or refrigerated overnight.

Unless stated otherwise, butter is the salted variety and the milk we used was 2%. Generally a mixer is used in these recipes. If a mixer is not a good idea, it is mentioned.

Buy an oven thermometer. This will give you a true reading of your oven's temperature. Over time, you may discover that it is different than what your oven temperature gauge claims it is.

We froze nearly all of our pastries at some stage of production. For the few that react poorly to being frozen, I have made note of the fact.

Keep in mind that these recipes are designed to work at high altitude and that preparing them at lower altitudes may require minor adjustments.

Recipes often call for very small amounts of lemon zest and the rest of the lemon often goes to waste. Zest the entire lemon. Measure what you need for the current recipe. Portion the remaining lemon rind, ½ teaspoon in each square of an ice cube tray and cover each portion with a ½ teaspoon of the lemon juice. Cover the tray with plastic and label it. Freeze for the next time a recipe calls for lemon zest. Use ice cube trays to freeze leftover apricot nectar also.

Chocolate melts much easier if it is in smaller pieces. If you buy bars of chocolate, break them up or chop them up before melting. Suggestions for leftover milk chocolate: use it to coat little bunches of roasted nuts, or pat any moisture off of a few fresh strawberries and dip them in the chocolate. Refrigerate the dipped strawberries for a couple of minutes to harden the chocolate.

Délice

In the spring of 1924, Walter Huber was born the seventh of what would be the ten surviving children of Ernst and Marie Huber. He grew up and attended school in a neighborhood of Bern, Switzerland known as the Felsenau, nestled in a bend of the Aare river.

Huber family home, Felsenau, Switzerland

As a very young man, Walter's family squelched his hopes of a higher education with their sentiments of "Why should you have something none of us had?". He worked jobs such as dishwasher, factory worker and vineyard worker, which held little promise of a future. Eventually his enthusiasm at a job at a fine confiserie, or confectionery shop, in Bern inspired the owner to arrange an apprenticeship for him in a pastry shop in Geneva. After two years in apprenticeship Walter reached the age of 20, which meant that his compulsory Swiss Army training began. Since it was the summer of 1944, he was not released back to his apprenticeship until an end was declared to World War II. There were a number of difficult times during Walter's apprenticeship, but he eventually passed the state-monitored exams with flying colors.

Over the following eight years, Walter honed his skills and collected pastry recipes by working in a number of Swiss resorts. In 1956, a chef that he had worked with at one of these resorts suddenly sent him a postcard from the United States, encouraging him to make the trip. Lacking the funds for the journey, Walter accepted a pastry chef position at Chicago's Drake Hotel in exchange for passage to the United States via the Queen Mary.

Lenk, Switzerland, 1947

Walter in Nyon, Switzerland, 1946

After five months in America, Walter was not enjoying Chicago and so was easily tempted by a fellow Swiss chef to leave the Drake Hotel to become the pastry chef at Aspen's Hotel Jerome. After a year in the position, a local banker saw promise in the 32-year-old and suggested that he start his own place, with a loan from the bank. (That would never have happened if Walter had stayed in Switzerland.) The very first Délice restaurant opened in a small ground level space in the Golden Horn building in 1957 Aspen. It offered a selection of European pastries, chocolates and candies, besides a small luncheon menu.

In 1960 the building was under contract to sell, so Walter quickly purchased the Tiedeman's store building just around the corner on Hyman Street, a half a block east of the Wheeler Opera House. The old building was razed except for portions of the foundation. In its place, a two-story red brick building with a full basement was built. The top floor was living quarters with a small deck that extended out to the alley in the back, which very nicely doubled as a carport for the Willy's Jeep (Walter's first car). The ground floor was a kitchen and dishwashing station in the back and service

Viola and a co-worker, 1959

counter and 4 or 5 small tables in the front. The basement was divided into a large walk-in refrigerator and two storage rooms, one for perishables and one for paper goods and cases of Swiss chocolates and candies. (There are many fond childhood memories of secretly appropriating chocolates and candies from that rock-walled room.)

Amidst the building process, Walter managed to court and propose to Viola Kinne, a nurse at the Pitkin County Hospital. Viola had arrived in Aspen from Bloomington, Illinois in search of good skiing, after learning to ski in Yosemite, California. The two were introduced to each other by a mutual Swiss friend, Paul Wirth, who then ran and lived at the Sundeck restaurant at the top of Ajax Mountain. Walter made the wedding cake and it went with the two of them over the gravel road of Independence Pass to Illinois for an October wedding. The honeymoon was switched at the last minute from Yucatan, Mexico to New Orleans when business expenses were more than expected.

In 1962 Walter passed the U.S. citizenship exam and was sworn in at a small ceremony in Glenwood Springs, along with four other European-born Aspenites. Over the next four years, two daughters arrived, first Cynthia (Cindy), then Vreneli (Vreni), and the family moved their living quarters to a new house in Starwood. (That was long before anyone famous lived there.) With access created by the construction of a new staircase in the front of the shop, the upstairs of the business building was converted into dining space. A dumbwaiter was installed to move the bus tubs filled with dirty dishes to the ground floor. (It seemed like such a modern idea to us kids.)

With the help of many friends and occasionally family members, the Délice came to thrive. The highlight of each winter season was entry in the January Winterskol Parade, followed by the torchlight decent and fireworks on Ajax Mountain.

Walter made his first attempt at retirement in 1975; selling the building to enjoy a life of leisure. Boredom quickly set in and he accepted a job working for Paul Wirth at Sam's Knob, the restaurant at the top of the Snowmass ski area. Viola went back to work at the hospital. Walter never skiied again after that winter.

The new building in Aspen, 1960

Délice

The third incarnation of the Délice started the following year in a rented space in the newly constructed Mason & Morse building, overlooking Wagner Park and the ski slopes of Ajax. The baking and most of the food production was done in a large kitchen at the Airport Business Center. The food was then driven to the downtown location. This arrangement lasted into early 1978, when the business was purchased by two Swiss chefs who had worked at The Red Onion.

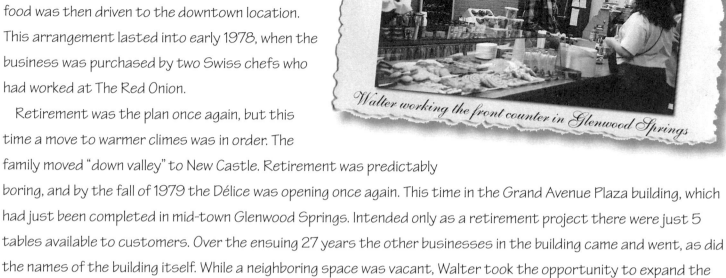

Walter working the front counter in Glenwood Springs

Retirement was the plan once again, but this time a move to warmer climes was in order. The family moved "down valley" to New Castle. Retirement was predictably boring, and by the fall of 1979 the Délice was opening once again. This time in the Grand Avenue Plaza building, which had just been completed in mid-town Glenwood Springs. Intended only as a retirement project there were just 5 tables available to customers. Over the ensuing 27 years the other businesses in the building came and went, as did the names of the building itself. While a neighboring space was vacant, Walter took the opportunity to expand the dining room. The walls in the additional room became a display area for Viola's creative crafts and sewing projects, often including a full size quilt.

By the spring of 2006, a lengthy list of forces at work at both the local and national levels had all coalesced to make keeping the restaurant open in Glenwood Springs an increasingly stressful experience. Health and personality issues also played a role in the equation. In the end, the situation had become so impossible that when another employee gave notice, the decision to close the doors after nearly 50 years took just a minute or two to make. Ironically, Friday, May 26th, 2006, the very last day, was the busiest day in the entire history of the restaurant.

The final day

Délice _____

Introduction

After working on this book for over two years, a former customer asked me why I was doing it. At the time, the question took me completely by surprise, but it certainly set me to thinking about my motivations. Despite a very deep connection with the place, I had sworn when I left for college that I would never "get stuck working at the shop". When I came back to work at the restaurant after college graduation, I swore that it would "just be for a few months". Eighteen years later, when we closed the restaurant, I was still there.

"The Shop", as we called The Délice, was where the Huber family came together; all of us were there over the course of each week, either working or just dropping by for something to eat. When the help didn't show up, or a rockslide or a forest fire prevented one of us from traveling to work, another of us rearranged their schedule to fill the void. "The Shop" is where we got weekly updates, not just on our lives, but also on those of the customers, some of which we had been serving food to for generations, literally. When we closed the doors of the Glenwood Springs location in May of 2006, we were serving the grandchildren of the customers and former employees of the original store in Aspen.

When Walter was trained in the pastry traditions of Switzerland, the golden rule was that recipes were secret. The only way to learn new recipes was to work in a position where you had to learn and use them. The pastry recipes that we used were ones that Walter had collected by working in a number of Swiss resorts following his formal apprenticeship in Geneva. Walter also sincerely believed that if everyone had access to our recipes, they would be much less likely to eat at the restaurant. Walter had organized two cookbooks over the decades, but neither had included recipes for any of the luncheon foods and, as was the fashion of the day, both books assumed that the reader was quite comfortable in a kitchen.

Once the restaurant doors were closed for good, there was no longer any reason not to share all of our recipes. This project has combined my lifelong desire to write, with my sincere desire for anyone to be able to create these wonderful foods at home. I have come to realize that The Délice restaurant, in its four incarnations, was not just a place to eat, it was where people came together. This book is my way of keeping a lifetime of memories of food and friends alive.

Glossary

almond meal or flour – available in the health food section at the local grocery. If not, you can create it by grinding blanched almonds into a fine meal with a food processor.
A courser version can be made by rolling blanched almonds on a cutting board with a rolling pin. One cup of sliced almonds will result in approximately ¾ cup of meal.

double boiler – a method of indirect heating on a stove by placing a bowl or pan over a smaller pan that is partially filled with water. The upper bowl or pan should not actually touch the water in the smaller pan, but sit over it.

eggwash – an egg that has been stirred with a small wire whip or fork, generally used to brush the top of dough with in order to get a shiny, pretty finish.

jagger – fancy cousin to a pizza cutter; a wheeled cutting tool that while cutting, leaves a "pinked" or serrated edge.

lemon zest – the outermost yellow portion of the lemon rind that is generally finely grated for use. (see Notes)

pastry bag – cone-shaped plastic or cloth "bag" used to squeeze decorative frostings or fillings into place; cake decorating tube.

rolling surface – any countertop, table or improvised surface where there is room enough to roll a dough out.

to pipe – to use a pastry or decorating bag, or any functional substitute for one, to squeeze some type of edible substance onto a baking sheet or other surface.

Conversion Chart

⅓ tablespoon = 1 teaspoon
½ tablespoon = 1 ½ teaspoons
1 tablespoon = 3 teaspoons

¼ cup = 4 tablespoons
⅓ cup = 5 tablespoons + 1 teaspoon
½ cup = 8 tablespoons
¾ cup = 12 tablespoons
1 cup = 16 tablespoons

1 cup = ½ pint
2 cups = 1 pint

Délice

Table of Contents

SELECTED PASTRY RECIPES

from

DÉLICE

CONTINENTAL PASTRY SHOP
AND TEA ROOM

Aspen, Colorado

The first Delice recipebook, 1972

Whole Wheat Bread (page 29),
French Bread and Rolls (page 27)

Mark Hatch Photography

Holiday Butter & Egg Bread
(page 34), Stollen (page 36)

Mark Hatch Photography

Breakfast Danish
(page 31)

Clockwise from foreground: Sable or Pinwheel (page 75), Cream Cheese Bar (page 89), Lemon & Rasberry Shells (page 78), Palette (page 64)

Vanilla Holiday Meringues (page 84)

Cherry Cream Cheese "Pizza" Pie (page 58), Apple Strudel (page 54)

Clockwise from foreground: Chocolate Square (page 65), Leckerle (page 90), Almond Cinnamon Shortbread (page 79)

Grandma Kinne's Rhubarb Custard Pie (page 95)

Butterfly (page 50), Bowtie (page 52)

Chocolate Sparrows (page 66)

Linzer Torte (page 91)

Half Moon, Linzer Bars,
Linzer Cookies (see Linzer
Torte, page 91)

Clockwise from foreground: French Nougat (page 77), Coconut Macaroon (page 73), Half Moon (see Linzer Torte, page 91), Walnut Bar (page 94)

Rasberry Mousse "Cake" (page 82)

Chocolate Eclair , Cream Puff (page 80), Chocolate Mousse (page 82)

19

Mocca Cake (page 104), topped with chocolate sprinkles

Mocca Squares (page 106)

Mocca Cake (page 104), topped with drizzled chocolate

Clockwise from foreground: Peppermint
Square (page 64), Sarah Bernhardt (page 60),
Rumball (page 63), Hotdog (page 84),
Ragusa (page 67), Cornet (page 73)

Black Forest Cake (page 100)

Napoleans (page 56)

Lemony Raspberry Cheesecake
(page 96), Pecan Pie (page 94)

Clockwise from foreground:
Viennese Wafer (page 88), Florentines
(page 61), Lemon Boats (page 76),
Almond Macaroon (page 72)

Gingerbread cookies
(page 112), Poppyseed
Poundcake (page 79)

Chocolate Coated
Candied Nuts (page 69)

Gingerbread House (page 113)

Meringue Mushrooms (page 85)

The last tray of pastries at the retirement party

The Breads

I have always wondered about the mystique of bread baking and the fear
it seems to engender in people, even those who feel very comfortable in a
kitchen. Walter, and in turn all of us who worked at the Délice, never had any
formal training in bread baking and we did just fine. French Bread is truly an
especially simple process and does not require a great deal of time to create,
and the rewards are well worth the small amount of effort. It does take some
time for the bread to rise and bake, but if you're going to be home anyway,
why not take the ten or fifteen minutes to mix up the dough. The trick is
remembering to prepare the sponge ahead of time. If I'm going to be creating
the bread in the morning, I mix the sponge before I go to bed the night before.
If evening is going to fit into my schedule better, I prepare the sponge in the
morning before heading off to work. It only takes a few minutes.

Breads and Rolls

Vreni and Cindy with "bread babies"

Délice

FRENCH BREAD

I have tried to recreate Walter's wonderful French bread as best I can. Honestly I think that the secret was in the type of flour that we used (Con Agra's Minnesota Girl) that is not available at the local grocery store. After much testing I have discovered that the flours labeled "better for bread" result in a bread closer in texture to the original, yet all-purpose flour will work just fine. The best texture is created by using half all-purpose and half bread flour.

Makes 1 loaf or 10-12 rolls.

10 to 14 hours before you intend to actually make the bread, prepare a sponge:

2 tablespoons active dry yeast
¾ cup water - warm to the touch, but not hot (105°-115°)
1-¼ cups bread and/or all-purpose flour

If you have a mixer that has a dough hook, use it. If not, mix the sponge with a sturdy spoon. Be sure that the bowl that you choose is roomy enough to allow the sponge to rise to about double its initial size. In the bowl, mix the yeast with the warm water. Add the flour and mix until the ingredients form a sticky dough. Cover the bowl with plastic and let it sit at room temperature until you are ready to make the bread. (It will rise and fall while it sits.)

Prepare an eggwash (see Glossary) and set aside.

1 cup water (warm to the touch, but not hot)
2-¾ cups bread and/or all-purpose flour
2-¼ teaspoons salt

Preheat oven to 400°.

If you have a mixer with a dough hook:
To the sponge, add the additional warm water, the flour and the salt and mix until a dough is formed. Let the dough mix for five to seven minutes. Scrape the dough onto a floured surface (preferably wooden). Dust lightly with more flour. Knead the dough by folding it over and pressing it down with the palms of your hands, turning it a quarter turn and repeating the process 6-10 times. Dust the dough and your fingers with flour if it is sticking to your hands.

If you are doing this by hand:
To the sponge, add the additional warm water, the flour and the salt and mix it together using a sturdy spoon. Once it begins to ball up, abandon the spoon and use your hands to knead the dough to incorporate all the flour. Scrape the dough onto a floured surface (preferably wooden). Dust the dough lightly with more flour. Knead the dough by folding it over and pressing it down with the palms of your hands, turning it a quarter turn and repeating the process for eight to ten minutes. Dust the dough and your fingers with flour if it is sticking to your hands.

Both methods:
At this point you have choices. You can roll the dough into a single loaf by rolling it and tucking the underside of the dough up into itself and then using your fingers to square the ends until it is shaped like a log. Pinch the seam together to be sure that the loaf will not unravel when it begins to rise. You can cut the dough in half and make two small loaves or roll the two halves into long, thin baguettes using the same technique.

Whatever your choice, place the shaped dough onto a parchment lined baking sheet. Use a pastry brush or your fingers to lightly coat the top of the dough with eggwash; then use a knife to make several small, shallow slits at an angle across the top.

Your other choice is to make 10-12 rolls with the dough. Cut the dough into roughly even pieces. To roll each piece, place your hand over it and curve your fingers around it and roll it in place while pressing in a downward motion. This technique may take practice to master, but keep trying. If this doesn't work initially, simply tuck the piece of dough underneath all around. Place the rolls on a parchment lined baking sheet; brush them with eggwash; and then use a knife to cut them deeply across the middle (nearly in half). For hamburger buns simply omit the cut.

continued on next page...

Délice

FRENCH BREAD cont.

Proofing is the process of encouraging the dough to rise. We had a special cabinet, called a proof cabinet, in which to do this, but sitting the dough anywhere warm (and moist, if possible) will do.* Avoid drafty places that can cause a crust to form over the bread, preventing it from rising to it's full potential. Let the dough rise until it is half again as big. How long this will take is completely dependent on the air temperature and humidity. If it begins to develop stretch marks, put it in the oven. Place the risen dough into the preheated oven carefully so as not to have it collapse.

Bake a single loaf for 25-30 minutes, turning the tray once to assure even browning. Bake rolls for 10 minutes, turn the tray around in the oven, and bake for another 8-10 minutes. The bread is done when the bottom of it has some color. Resist the temptation to cut the bread until it has cooled for 20-30 minutes.

*Cynthia's Note: I place my water-filled teapot on one of the stove burners and let it simmer on low heat to add moisture to the air. I then sit the tray of rising bread on the nearby burners where the preheating oven below the stove creates warmth.

Passing out Delice coffee mugs

Délice

WHOLE WHEAT BREAD

We made this bread each morning by cutting off a big hunk of the French bread dough, tossing it back into the mixer and adding the wheat flour. It tends to be a softer bread, lacking the crust that the French bread develops. If it is available, the "better for bread" flours do work better for the white flour, but all-purpose will work just fine.

Makes 1 loaf or 10-12 rolls.

10 to 14 hours before you intend to actually make the bread, prepare a sponge:

2 tablespoons active dry yeast
¾ cup water - warm to the touch, but not hot (105°-115°)
1-¼ cups white bread flour

If you have a mixer that has a dough hook, use it. If not, mix the sponge with a sturdy spoon. Be sure that the bowl that you choose is roomy enough to allow the sponge to rise to about double its initial size. In the bowl, mix the yeast with the warm water. Add the flour and mix until the ingredients form a sticky dough. Cover the bowl with plastic and let it sit at room temperature until you are ready to make the bread. (It will rise and fall while it sits.)

Prepare an eggwash (see Glossary) and set aside.

1 cup water (warm to the touch, but not hot)
¾ cup white bread flour
1-½ cups whole wheat flour
2-¼ teaspoons salt

Preheat oven to 400°.

If you have a mixer with a dough hook:
To the sponge, add the additional warm water, the white flour, the whole wheat flour and the salt and mix until a dough is formed. Let the dough mix for several minutes. Scrape the dough onto a surface (preferably wooden) dusted with wheat flour. Dust the dough lightly with more wheat flour. Knead it by folding it over and pressing it down with the palms of your hands, turning it a quarter turn and repeating the process 6-10 times. Dust the dough and your fingers with the wheat flour if it is sticking to your hands.

If you are doing this by hand:
To the sponge, add the additional warm water, the white flour, the whole wheat flour and the salt and mix it together using a sturdy spoon. Once it begins to ball up, abandon the spoon and use your hands to knead the dough to incorporate all the flour. Scrape the dough onto a floured surface (preferably wooden). Dust the dough lightly with more flour. Knead the dough by folding it over and pressing it down with the palms of your hands, turning it a quarter turn and repeating the process for eight to ten minutes. Dust the dough and your fingers with flour if it is sticking to your hands.

Both methods:
At this point you have choices. You can roll the dough into a single loaf by rolling it and tucking the underside of the dough up into itself and then using your fingers to square the ends until it is shaped like a log. Pinch the seam together to be sure that the loaf will not unravel when it begins to rise. You can cut the dough in half and make two small loaves or roll the two halves into long, thin baguettes using the same technique.

Whatever your choice, place the shaped dough on a parchment lined baking sheet, seam side down. Use a pastry brush or your fingers to coat the top with eggwash and then dust the top with a bit of wheat flour.

Your other choice is to make 10-12 rolls with the dough. Cut the dough into roughly even pieces. To roll each piece, place your hand over it and curve your fingers around it and roll it in place while pressing in a downward motion. This technique may take practice to master, but keep trying. If this doesn't work initially, simply tuck the piece of dough underneath all around. Place the rolls on a parchment lined baking sheet, brush them with eggwash, and dust each one with a bit of wheat flour.

continued on next page...

Délice _____

WHOLE WHEAT BREAD cont.

Proofing is the process of encouraging the dough to rise. We had a special cabinet in which to do this, but sitting the dough anywhere warm (and moist, if possible) will do.* Avoid drafty places that can cause a crust to form over the bread, preventing it from rising to it's full potential. Let the dough rise until it is half again as big. How long this will take is completely dependent on the air temperature and humidity. If it begins to develop stretch marks, put it in the oven. Place the risen dough into the preheated oven carefully so as not to have it collapse.

Bake a single loaf for 25-30 minutes, turning the tray once to assure even browning. Bake rolls for 10 minutes, turn the tray around in the oven, and bake for another 8-10 minutes. The bread is done when the bottom of it has some color. Resist the temptation to cut the bread until it has cooled for 20-30 minutes.

*Cynthia's Note: I place my water-filled teapot on one of the stove burners and let it simmer on low heat to add moisture to the air. I then sit the tray of rising bread on the nearby burners where the preheating oven creates warmth.

The Winterskol Parade, 1963

Délice

BREAKFAST DANISH

The cinnamon rolls were often requested even years after we discontinued their production. Besides being the ultimate breakfast treat, they make a very tasty dessert after dinner. For those readers who remember the days in Aspen, I have included the cream cheese and almond filling as well. This is a recipe that is best done without the aid of a mixer.

Makes 20 very small rolls or 12 larger ones.

Prepare the Apricot Sugar Glaze recipe (page 42) and set aside or refrigerate.

5-½ tablespoons butter
5-½ tablespoons margarine
1-¾ cups all-purpose flour
1-½ tablespoons active dry yeast
3 tablespoons water - warm to the touch,
  but not hot (105°-115°)
½ cup milk
pinch of malted milk powder (optional)
½ teaspoon salt
3-½ teaspoons sugar
1 egg

Fillings:
½ cup light brown sugar
1-½ teaspoons ground cinnamon
raisins (optional)

or

8 ounces soft cream cheese – room temperature is
  much easier to spread
¼ cup chopped roasted almonds

Let the butter and margarine reach room temperature. Measure the flour and set it aside. In a large mixing bowl, use a wire whip to mix the yeast and the warm water. Heat the milk until it is just warm to the touch and add it to the yeast mixture. This can be done in a saucepan on low heat for 2-3 minutes or by microwaving it in intervals of 5-10 seconds. Should you accidentally overheat it, wait until it cools back down before pouring it into the yeast mixture, as too high a temperature will kill the yeast. Stir in the malted milk powder, the salt, the sugar and the egg. With a sturdy spoon, stir the flour in, only until it is dampened. (The rolling process will complete the mixing.)

Onto a well-floured board or countertop, scrape the sticky dough and press it into a rectangular shape about a half-inch thick. If the butter is still cold, use your hands to "massage" the butter on a cutting board until it is well-softened or cream it with the margarine in a mixer on low speed. Using your fingers or a spatula, spread both the softened butter and the margarine onto 2/3rds of the dough. **(A)** Fold the unbuttered third over half of the buttered portion, then fold the remaining third over the top. This should result in a rectangular dough one third the size of the original with a layer of butter between each layer of dough. **(B)** Being sure to keep the surface below the dough well-floured **(C)** and the rectangular shape maintained, roll the dough until it is roughly an 11 x 19 inch rectangle. Fold the dough in thirds using the short edges and roll once more. Place the dough into the refrigerator to rest for 2 or more hours or overnight.

continued on next page...

A

B

BREAKFAST DANISH cont.

Preheat oven to 350°.

Again, on a well-floured surface, roll the dough out until it is a half-inch thick (approximately 11 x 19 inches). Fold by thirds, using the short ends, and roll one last time. For large rolls, moisten a half-inch of the dough on one long edge with water or eggwash. For smaller rolls, cut the rectangle in half lengthwise, moisten a long edge on both pieces. **(D)** For cinnamon danish, mix the cinnamon into the brown sugar and spread it over all of the dough except the moistened edge(s). Sprinkle with raisins if desired. For cream cheese/almond danish, spread the cream cheese over the dough except for the moistened edge(s) and sprinkle with the roasted almonds. **(E)**

Fold the long edge opposite the moistened seam over the filling, and continue rolling it to create a "cake roll". **(F)** Cut the "cake roll(s)" into 1-½ inch sections and place the sections, cut side down, onto a baking sheet **(G)** (if you wish for a loaf effect place 5 or 6 of them into a pie or cake pan.)

Proofing is the process of encouraging the dough to rise. Anywhere warm (and moist, if possible) will do.* Avoid drafty places that can cause a crust to form over the dough, preventing it from rising to it's full potential. Let the dough rise until it is half again as big. How long this will take is completely dependent on the air temperature and humidity.

Bake small rolls 12-16 minutes, large rolls 17-20 minutes or until the rolls are nicely browned on top. Brush with the apricot sugar glaze immediately upon removal from the oven.

*Cynthia's Note: I place my water-filled teapot on one of the stove burners and let it simmer on low heat to add moisture to the air. I then sit the tray of rising danish on the nearby burners where the preheating oven below the stove creates warmth.

C

D

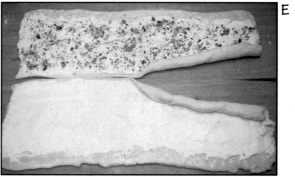
E

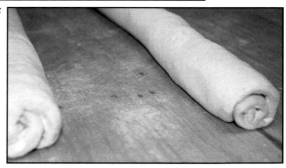
F

G

Délice

CROISSANT

In Europe, this flaky, buttery pastry is traditionally served with a selection of preserves or honey for breakfast. Instead, we used them to serve sandwiches on. If it is available, high-gluten flour will give a truer texture.

Makes 8 small croissants.

Prepare an eggwash (see Glossary) and refrigerate.

4 tablespoons butter
1-⅓ cups all-purpose flour (or high-gluten)
1 tablespoon active dry yeast
2 tablespoons warm water (105°-115°)
½ cup milk
pinch of malted milk powder (optional)
½ teaspoon salt
2-½ teaspoons sugar

Ideally, let the butter reach room temperature. Measure the flour and set aside. In a large mixing bowl, use a wire whip to mix the yeast and warm water. Heat the milk just until it is warm to the touch and add it to the yeast mixture. Should it become hot to the touch, cool it back down to merely warm before adding it to the yeast. Stir in the malted milk powder, the salt, and the sugar. With a sturdy spoon, stir the flour in, only until it is dampened. (The rolling process will complete the mixing.)

Onto a well-floured board or countertop, scrape the sticky dough and press it into a rectangular shape about a half-inch thick. If the butter is still cold, use your hands to "massage" the butter on a cutting board until it is well-softened or cream it in a mixer on low speed. Spread the softened butter onto 2/3rds of the dough. **(A)** Fold the unbuttered third over half of the buttered portion, then fold the remaining third over the top. **(B)** This should result in a rectangular dough one third the size of the original with a layer of butter between each layer of dough. **(C)**

Being sure to keep the surface below the dough well-floured and the rectangular shape maintained, roll the dough until it is roughly an 8 x 13 inch rectangle. Fold the dough in thirds. **(D)** Roll and fold the dough in thirds once more. Place the folded dough into the refrigerator to rest for at least 2 hours or overnight.

Preheat oven to 350°.

Again, on a well-floured surface, roll the dough out into a roughly 8 x 13 inch rectangle. Fold by thirds and roll one last time. Cut the dough in half lengthwise. Cut the two resulting strips into rough triangles. Roll each triangle toward one point **(E)** and place on a parchment lined baking sheet. Brush the top of each croissant lightly with the eggwash.

Proofing is the process of encouraging the dough to rise. We had a special cabinet, called a proof cabinet, in which to do this, but sitting it anywhere warm (and moist, if possible) will do.* Avoid drafty places that can cause a crust to form over the dough, preventing it from rising to it's full potential. Let the croissants rise until they are half again as big. How long this will take is completely dependent on the air temperature and humidity.

Bake 15-17 minutes or until browned lightly underneath (not just on the top).

*Cynthia's Note: I place my water-filled teapot on one of the stove burners and let it simmer on low heat to add moisture to the air. I then sit the tray of croissants on the nearby burners where the preheating oven below the stove creates warmth.

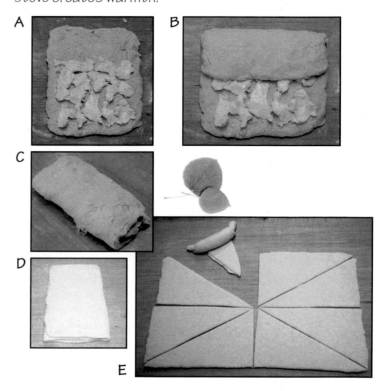

HOLIDAY BUTTER AND EGG BREAD

The Swiss-German name for this braided bread is zopf. We only prepared it in the days prior to Thanksgiving, Christmas and Easter, which meant that even we considered it a real treat. Each batch resulted in one loaf that was undersized, which we often consumed within minutes of it being cool enough to slice. This bread freezes nicely. It is the tastiest choice for the sandwiches made with holiday leftovers. The best texture is produced by using half bread flour and half all-purpose flour, but it is still delectable if made with just one kind.

Makes 1 large or 2 small braided loaves.

Prepare an eggwash (see Glossary) and refrigerate.

3 tablespoons butter
3 tablespoons margarine
1 tablespoon active dry yeast
1 tablespoon warm water
1 cup whole milk, divided
3-½ cups bread or all-purpose flour, divided
¼ teaspoon malted milk powder (optional)
¼ teaspoon vanilla
2 eggs
1-¼ teaspoons salt

Let the butter, the margarine and the eggs reach room temperature (leave out overnight if necessary). Should you forget, once you have added the butter, the margarine and the eggs to the other ingredients, let them all sit an additional half an hour.

If you have a mixer with a dough hook, take advantage of it. If not, use an oversized bowl and a sturdy spoon. In the bowl, use a fork to crudely stir together the yeast and the warm water. Warm ½ cup of the milk until it is just warm to your fingertips. This can be done in a saucepan on low heat for 2-3 minutes or by microwaving it in intervals of 5-10 seconds. Should you accidentally overheat it, wait until it cools back down before pouring it into the yeast mixture, as too high a temperature will kill the yeast. Use the whip or fork to crudely mix the milk into the yeast mixture. Add 1 cup of the flour and use a dough hook or spoon to mix for a couple of minutes.

Into the bowl with the yeast/flour mixture, add, but do not mix, the malted milk powder, the vanilla, and the eggs. Cut the butter and the margarine into 3-4 pieces each and add them also. DO NOT stir it. Warm the remaining ½ cup of the milk and pour it over the bowl's contents. Cover the bowl with plastic and let it sit at room temperature for 2 hours. Measure 2-½ cups of flour and the salt and set them aside (if using just all-purpose flour measure an additional 2 tablespoons).

Preheat oven to 375º.

Line a baking sheet with parchment paper. Uncover the bowl. Add the measured flour and the salt and mix for 5-7 minutes. A dough will form. Lightly flour a rolling surface and scrape the dough onto it. Dust the dough with flour and knead it for a minute or two, dusting it with flour as needed to keep it from sticking to your hands. Roll it into a crude log shape.

To braid the dough, cut the dough in half lengthwise. **(A)** Using both hands, roll each half into a long narrow "snake". Place one "snake" pointing directly away from you. Lay the other perpendicular across the middle of the first. **(B)** Taking one end of the first "snake" in each hand, cross your hands, right over left. **(C)** Drop the ends. Pick up the ends of the other "snake" and cross them, left hand over right. **(D)** Continue this pattern until you just have the very tips left. **(E) + (F)** Press the tips together and tuck them underneath the loaf. **(G)** If two smaller loaves will work better, cut the dough into two pieces, then each piece into two halves. Braid each half of the dough separately. If the braiding is just too much, simply roll the dough into a log shape, being sure to tuck the dough up into the bottom to create some tension across the top. Place the loaf or loaves onto the parchment lined sheet. **(H)** Brush the top with eggwash and use a pair of scissors to snip 4-5 small cuts into the top. (This allows the dough to expand.)

Délice

HOLIDAY BUTTER AND EGG BREAD cont.

Proofing is the process of encouraging the dough to rise. We had a special cabinet, called a proof cabinet, in which to do this, but sitting it anywhere warm (and moist, if possible) will do.* Avoid drafty places that can cause a crust to form over the bread, preventing it from rising to its full potential. Let the dough rise until it is half again as big. How long this will take is completely dependent on the air temperature and humidity. If it begins to tear, put it in the oven.

Bake the bread for 20-25 minutes, turning it around once if your oven tends to bake unevenly. Resist the temptation to slice it until it's rested for 15-20 minutes.

*Cynthia's Note: I place my water-filled teapot on one of the stove burners and let it simmer on low heat to add moisture to the air. I then sit the tray of rising bread on the nearby burners where the preheating oven below the stove creates warmth.

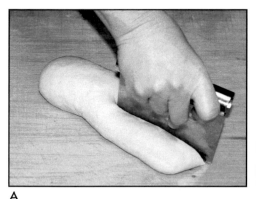

A

B

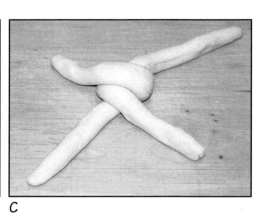

C

D

E

F

G

H

Délice _____

STOLLEN (pronounced shto'-len)

Reserved for the holiday season, we only had these sweet loaves available in the freezer showcase from Thanksgiving through Christmas. Sweet, but not overly so, slices of stollen are great for breakfast or as dessert.

Use half all-purpose flour and half bread flour for an ideal texture. Fruit cake mix is generally only available during the holiday season, so purchase extra and keep it frozen.

Makes three (3 x 5 inch) loaves.

Prepare the Apricot Sugar Glaze recipe (page 42). Set it aside or refrigerate.

4 tablespoons + 2 teaspoons butter, divided
8 tablespoons margarine
½ cup candied fruit (fruit cake mix)
½ teaspoon dark rum
½ cup raisins
2 tablespoons sugar
2-¾ cups bread or all-purpose flour, divided
1 tablespoon + ½ teaspoon active dry yeast
2 tablespoons warm water
1 cup whole milk, divided
¾ teaspoon salt
¼ teaspoon malted milk powder (optional)
¼ teaspoon vanilla
1 tablespoon honey
⅓ cup roasted, sliced almonds, divided

Let 4 tablespoons of butter and the margarine reach room temperature (leave out overnight if necessary). In a small bowl, stir the rum into the candied fruit, cover with plastic and let steep while the butter and margarine warm.

Measure and set aside the raisins and then the sugar. Measure 1-¼ cups of the flour and set it aside.

If you have a mixer with a dough hook, take this opportunity to use it. If not, use an oversized bowl and a sturdy spoon. In the appropriate bowl, use a fork to crudely stir together the yeast and the warm water. Warm ½ cup of the milk until it is really warm to your fingertips. This can be done in a saucepan on low heat

for 2-3 minutes or by microwaving it in intervals of 5-10 seconds. Should you accidentally overheat it, wait until it cools back down before pouring it into the yeast mixture, as too high a temperature will kill the yeast. Once you have added the warmed milk, add the flour that you had measured and set aside. Mix it in for a couple of minutes. While it is mixing, measure 1-½ cups of flour and the salt and set them aside.

Into the mixer bowl with the yeast mixture, add, but do not stir, the rum-laced candied fruit, raisins, sugar, malted milk powder, vanilla, and honey. Cut 4 tablespoons of the butter and all of the margarine into tablespoon-size chunks and add them also. Warm the remaining ½ cup of milk and pour it over the bowl's contents. DO NOT stir it. Cover the bowl with plastic and let it sit and rise at room temperature for at least 1 hour (30 minutes longer if the butter and margarine are cold).

Preheat oven to 325°.

Grease three 3 x 5 inch loaf pans. If the sliced almonds are not already roasted, use the preheating oven to roast them in a metal baking pan just until they begin to brown. The amount of time needed will vary greatly depending on the oven, but roughly 8-15 minutes. Set aside a tablespoon of the roasted almonds to sprinkle over the tops of the finished loaves.

Remove the plastic cover from the mixing bowl. Add the 1-½ cups of flour, the salt and ¼ cup of the roasted almonds and mix or knead for 5-7 minutes. Lightly flour a rolling surface and scrape the dough onto it. Dust the dough and your hands with flour as needed to keep from sticking and knead the dough for a minute or two. Cut the dough into three equal portions. Roll each portion into a "sausage" and place into the loaf pans.

Délice

Proofing is the process of encouraging the dough to rise. We had a special cabinet, called a proof cabinet, in which to do this, but sitting it anywhere warm (and moist, if possible) will do.* Avoid drafty places that can cause a crust to form over the bread, preventing it from rising to it's full potential. Let the dough rise until it is half again as big. How long this will take is completely dependent on the air temperature and humidity.

Bake the loaves for 25-30 minutes or until the tops are nicely brown. While they are baking, melt ¾ tablespoon of butter and stir it into 3 tablespoons of the apricot sugar glaze and again set it aside. Have a pastry brush handy. Upon removing the loaves from the oven, brush the top of each loaf with the buttery glaze. While the glaze is still warm, sprinkle the tablespoon of roasted almonds set aside earlier over the three loaves. Let the bread cool to room temperature before serving, refrigerating or freezing.

*Cynthia's proofing note: I place my water-filled teapot on one of the stove burners and let it simmer on low heat to add moisture to the air. I then sit the rising bread on the nearby burners where the preheating oven below the stove creates warmth.

Viola, the fashionable skier

The Delice at the Carbondale Mountain Fair

Our selection of nearly 30 different European-style pastries was what separated The Délice from all the other sandwich shops in town. We never gave up using the right ingredients, despite valiant efforts by wholesalers to get us to convert to bagged mixes. Real butter, real whipping cream, whole milk, and quality chocolate do make a difference.

Human nature is interesting to observe. We had two types of pastry customers. One that would get the exact same pastry on every visit, year after year. The other would try a different one each time and would be excited each time Walter came up with something new.

How does one shrink a recipe that made 32 cherry pizzas at a time? How do you measure a half of an egg? In converting our production-size recipes into recipes that could be used at home, several steps occurred. We weighed all our ingredients. So, first each recipe had to be converted from weights to cups and tablespoons. Then each recipe was downsized and tested until it really worked and was a size that made sense. As a result of this process, several of the recipes may seem to have very odd measurements.

The Pastries

*Canton shield of Bern,
Switzerland - black bear on a
yellow field with red corners*

Délice

Fillings, Glazes and Frostings

APRICOT SUGAR GLAZE

This is the glaze that we used on everything. We mixed it in a huge Hobart mixer using 22 pounds of powdered sugar at a time. We poured the glaze into plastic containers and kept them frozen, moving a container into the refrigerator as needed. Glaze will keep in the refrigerator for ages, but it spreads best if room temperature. If you don't think to take it out of the refrigerator until the last minute, a few seconds in the microwave will help.

Makes approximately ⅓ cup.

1-½ tablespoons apricot (or peach) nectar
1 tablespoon water
1 cup powdered sugar

In a saucepan or by using a microwave, heat the apricot nectar and the water just to boiling. Remove from heat and use a wire whip to stir in the powdered sugar. If it is too thick, add a few drops of hot water.

Use right away or allow the glaze to cool to room temperature before storing in an airtight container.

PLAIN SUGAR GLAZE

Glaze made in a hurry, or in the case of butterflies or bowties, brushed over a thin layer of heated apricot jam or syrup.

Makes ½ cup.

1 cup powdered sugar
1 tablespoon + 2 teaspoons hot water

In a bowl, use a wire whip to stir the hot water into the powdered sugar.

ROASTED ALMONDS

This is a basic outline for a small quantity of Roasted Almonds. It is perfectly okay to use a different oven temperature, if whichever recipe you are working on, calls for one. I even use my toaster oven occasionally, especially in the heat of summer. If you use more almonds, a larger pan, or a different oven temperature the roasting time will be different. Just keep a close eye on them; as the almonds near the edge of the pan darken, shake or stir them until they are evenly roasted. Be aware that once the almonds begin to brown it is only minutes before they will burn.

⅔ cup sliced almonds

Preheat oven to 350°.

Put almonds into a 9 x 5 inch loaf pan. Place in the oven for 6-9 minutes, shaking or stirring several times.

Let cool to room temperature before using or freezing.

ALMOND PASTE

This is a simple almond filling that we used for layering the Bowties, but it can also be used to fill small puffpastry turnovers or even Croissants. Although we used milk, you can substitute rum or kirschwasser (Swiss cherry brandy) for a more adult flavor. The almond meal too, can be replaced using the nut meal of your choice.

Makes approximately 2 cups.

1-½ cups almond meal or flour (see Glossary)
1 cup sugar
6 tablespoons milk

If you have not used roasted almonds to make your own almond meal, preheat oven or toaster oven to 350°. In a metal baking pan, roast the almond meal until it just begins to color around the edges (approximately 5-8 minutes). Stir the almond meal and continue to roast an additional 2 minutes. (Skip this roasting step if roasted almonds were used to make the almond meal.) Let the roasted almond meal cool to room temperature.

In a bowl, use a sturdy spoon to mix together the roasted almond meal, the sugar and 5 tablespoons of the milk. Add additional milk ½ teaspoon at a time only until the whole is a thick paste. Use right away or refrigerate or freeze for later use.

Délice

CUSTARD CREAM

Custard cream is the traditional filling for Napoleons and offers a tasty base for fruit tarts. It is so good though that you'll have a hard time to keep from simply eating it out of the pan.

1-1/3 cups milk
1/3 cup sugar
1 teaspoon vanilla
1 egg
3 tablespoons corn starch

Into a large saucepan, pour all but ½ cup of the milk. Use a wire whip to stir the sugar and the vanilla into the milk in the pan and set it aside. Into the remaining ½ cup of milk, whisk the egg and the corn starch and set aside.

Bring the contents of the saucepan to a boil over medium heat. When the milk begins to boil, whisk in the milk/egg/starch mixture. Stirring constantly, heat the cream over medium heat until it thickens. Remove from heat and let it cool to a temperature that will no longer burn your fingers before using.

*Narcissa Reeder, Aspen
employee for 14 years*

LEMON CREME

This lemon lover's delight was the basis for all of our lemon desserts, such as the addictive Lemon Boats and Almond Macaroons. Create a delicious cake frosting or filling for layering Poppyseed Poundcake, by whipping lemon creme with unsalted butter (5-½ tablespoons of butter for each cup of Lemon Creme).

Makes approximately 2 cups.

4 eggs
1 cup + 3 tablespoons sugar
1 small lemon
3 tablespoons butter
6-½ tablespoons margarine

Open and beat the eggs. Set them aside. Put the sugar into a bowl. Onto the sugar, finely grate the outermost yellow rind from the lemon. Cut the lemon in half and juice the lemon into a small bowl. Pour just 2 tablespoons of the juice into the sugar. Set the lemon sugar aside. Place the butter and margarine into a large saucepan and melt them over low heat. Add the lemon sugar to the pan. Increase the heat to medium. Use a wire whip to stir occasionally until the pan's contents reach a full boil. Add the eggs all at once and use the whip to stir constantly to prevent the mixture from attaching to the bottom of the pan. When the mixture reaches a full boil and begins to thicken a bit, remove it from the heat.

Being careful not to burn yourself, use a rubber spatula to force the creme through a wire strainer into a bowl. (Another option is to let it cool and squeeze it through cheesecloth.) Let the creme cool to room temperature before covering it with plastic and refrigerating it for at least 2 hours, or overnight, before using it. If you need it sooner, sit the bowl of lemon creme over a bowl of ice cubes until it is cool. Leftovers can be frozen in an airtight container for long periods.

CANACHE (pronounced gah' nahsh)

Walter's version of Canache is a blend of chocolates whipped with milk and butter to a light fluffy texture. Several of our more popular pastries, such as the Sarah Bernharts (more popularly known as Dolly Partons) and the Rumballs, are made from this tasty concoction. It is also the vital ingredient in the Peppermint Squares, Chocolate Squares and the Ragusa.

We always used high-quality Nestlé chocolate (called couverture) that came in very large 10 pound bars in combination with milk chocolate coating. For the best possible results, purchase chocolate with high levels of cocoa, but if you are willing to compromise the taste slightly, name-brand chocolate chips work well and melt quicker. If you prefer the flavor of the darker chocolate the way I do, simply use 5 ounces each of milk and dark chocolate instead of the traditional proportions. I offer two methods for the stovetop portion of the recipe. They work equally well, but the double-boiler method eliminates the chance of burning the chocolate.

Makes approximately 1-½ cups.

7 ounces milk chocolate or milk chocolate coating
   (1 cup chocolate chips)
3 ounces bittersweet or semi-sweet chocolate
   (a generous ½ cup chocolate chips)
¼ cup milk, half & half or heavy cream
2 tablespoons unsalted butter

If time allows, let the butter reach room temperature. Cut the chocolate into small chunks and set aside. (Omit this step if using chocolate chips.)

Important note: When working with chocolate, never ever, ever add water, either intentionally or even accidentally. Just a drop in the bowl can cause the entire thing to "freeze up".

The safer double boiler method:
Melt the chocolates together using a double boiler over medium heat, being sure that the upper bowl or pan is over the hot water and not in it. Meanwhile, heat the milk just until it begins to boil. This only takes a matter of minutes in a small saucepan over low to medium heat, or microwave the milk in 5-10 second intervals.

Pour the scalded milk into the chocolate and stir with a wire whip until smooth. Stir in the unsalted butter until smooth. Remove from heat and let cool to room temperature, then chill uncovered for at least an hour or even overnight.

In the saucepan method:
Heat the milk in a heavy saucepan just until it begins to bubble. Remove from the heat and use a wire whip to stir the chocolate and the butter in until it is smooth. Scrape into a bowl. Let cool to room temperature, then chill uncovered for at least an hour or even overnight.

Whipping it up:
Sit the bowl of canache over a pan of hot water (double boiler) until the edge of the chocolate begins to melt. Wipe the bottom of the bowl off with a towel to prevent any water dripping into the mixer bowl. Scrape the mixture into a mixing bowl. Starting with slow pulses, slowly increase the speed until you can whip the chocolate on high speed. Scrape the sides of the bowl often. The canache should lighten in color and become light and fluffy, BUT working with chocolate is all about temperature. Should the chocolate become liquidy, chill it right in the mixer bowl for five minutes and try again. If it remains too hard, sit the mixer bowl over hot water for a minute or two and try again. Several corrections may be needed. Once it works, use the canache right away as it will stiffen quickly. Any leftovers can be refrigerated or frozen in an airtight container for long periods of time and rewhipped as needed.

SOFT COOKIE DOUGH

This versatile Soft Cookie Dough was used to create the Shells, which we filled with either Lemon Creme or Raspberry Jam. This dough also constituted the "crust" for the Lemony Raspberry Cheesecakes and the Cream Cheese Bars. Although we never served this dough as simple cookies, we should have. For anyone with nut allergies, this is the answer.

2 cups cake flour
3 tablespoons butter
10 tablespoons margarine
½ teaspoon lemon zest
1 teaspoon lemon juice
½ cup sugar
¼ teaspoon vanilla
2-½ tablespoons milk
1 large egg

Preheat oven to 325°.

Measure and sift the flour and set aside. Melt just the butter. Cream the melted butter, the margarine, lemon rind, lemon juice, sugar and vanilla. Begin on low speed, scrape the bowl down at least once, then whip for a minute or two. Add the milk and the egg. Again, start on low speed, scrape the bowl down at least once, then whip for a couple of minutes until it is light and fluffy. Add the flour and mix on low speed just long enough to incorporate the flour. Do not overmix.

Follow directions for cheesecake crusts or shells.

VIENNESE WAFER DOUGH

This is a light almond dough that we used for Viennese Wafers, Lemon Boats, Chocolate Squares, Ragusa and even Pecan Pie and Grandma Kinne's Rhubarb Custard Pie.

3-½ cups cake flour
4 tablespoons (½ stick) butter
16 tablespoons (2 sticks) margarine
6 tablespoons sugar
5 tablespoons almond meal or flour (see Glossary)
½ cup milk
¼ teaspoon vanilla

Sift the flour and set aside. Melt just the butter. Cream together the melted butter, the margarine, the sugar and the almond flour. Scrape the bowl at least once. Once the ingredients are mixed, turn the mixer speed up to medium-high for a minute or two so that the mixture becomes light and fluffy. Scrape the mixture down into the bowl. Add the milk and the vanilla and mix, first on low speed, then on medium-high until light and fluffy again. Using only the lower mixer settings or, even better, using a rubber spatula to fold it in by hand, add the flour to the mixture. Mix only long enough to incorporate the flour; overmixing will result in a crumbly dough. The process of rolling the dough will finish the mixing. Place the rather sticky dough in a bowl and cover with plastic. Refrigerate for several hours or overnight before rolling.

This dough can be refrigerated for several days or frozen for long periods of time if wrapped well in plastic or in an airtight container.

CANDIED LEMON RIND

Any time we would juice a lemon without using the zest, we would freeze it to candy later. Although we only used the candied rind as an ingredient for Leckerle, small strips rolled in sugar or partially dipped in melted chocolate, can be served as a sweet treat. Store one candied lemon rind in the freezer and it will go a long way. If the process seems time consuming, chopped candied lemon rind is generally available at the local market during the holiday season (next to the fruit cake mix.) Buy a container and keep it frozen.

1 lemon
1 cup sugar
water

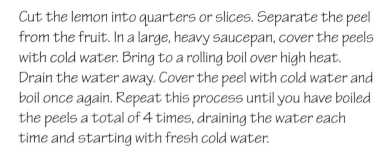

Cut the lemon into quarters or slices. Separate the peel from the fruit. In a large, heavy saucepan, cover the peels with cold water. Bring to a rolling boil over high heat. Drain the water away. Cover the peel with cold water and boil once again. Repeat this process until you have boiled the peels a total of 4 times, draining the water each time and starting with fresh cold water.

After draining the peel for the fourth time, add water once again until the peels are covered by at least one inch. Add the sugar and stir. Simmer over low heat until the syrup is nearly gone (be careful not to let it burn). Do not stir the syrup once it boils. If you need to move the peel around, swirl the pan. Use tongs to remove the peel to a piece of parchment to cool.

Store in an airtight container in the refrigerator for several weeks, or freeze.

ROYAL FROSTING

This is a classic cake decorating frosting that we used for decorating gingerbread people and assembling gingerbread houses. Once it is "dry" it is hard and fairly durable, if a bit brittle. While decorating, keep your mixing bowl covered with plastic or a damp towel to keep it from drying prematurely.

Makes approximately ⅔ cup of frosting.

1-¼ cup powdered sugar
2 tablespoons egg white (the white from 1 large egg)
½ teaspoon cream of tartar
½ teaspoon clear vanilla or almond extract (optional)

Whip all the ingredients 5-7 minutes until very white and fluffy. Ideally you want the frosting thick enough that it will hold a peak, but light enough to easily squeeze from a pastry tube or plastic bag. Adjust the consistency by using drops of water or tiny portions of egg white to thin it or adjust it the other way by adding one tablespoon of powdered sugar at a time.

Tint with drops of liquid or paste food color to add a seasonal twist.

Sandhill cranes dance on shades of light brown

Délice

Pastries Made with Puffpastry

PUFFPASTRY

Rolling the Puffpastry (or puffpaste) was considered an upper body workout, since the commercial recipe was 16 times as large as this one. Puffpastry is one of those foods that is a bit of work and takes time, but the reward is worth the effort. For those who either lack the time or the enthusiasm, it is now available in the frozen foods section of most grocery stores. For those who are willing, prepare to get your hands messy; this cannot be done in a mixer.

14 tablespoons margarine
8 tablespoons salted butter
3-¼ cups all purpose flour + enough to flour a rolling
   surface repeatedly
¼ slightly heaped teaspoon salt
1 cup + 1 tablespoon cold water

Let the butter and margarine reach room temperature.

Pour the flour and the salt into a large bowl and stir it with a fork just to mix. Cut 6 tablespoons of the margarine into 5 or 6 pieces and add to the bowl. Use your fingers to rub the flour and margarine together or use a pastry blender until the flour and margarine are roughly combined. Add the cup of cold water and stir with the fork until the water is incorporated. Add the tablespoon of cold water and use your hands to gently knead the dough only long enough to incorporate all the flour. Try not to use any more force than is necessary. Scrape the dough onto a lightly floured surface. Using the palm of your hand and your fingertips, shape the dough into a rectangle roughly 8 x 10 inches.

Place the remaining margarine and the butter in a bowl and use the fork to "squish" them together. Scrape the butter/margarine onto half of the dough and crudely even it out over just that half, leaving a ½ inch of the dough showing around the edge. **(A)** Fold the other half of the dough over the top of the butter/margarine to make a large "butter turnover". Use your fingertips to press the dough together around the edges. **(B)** Cover with plastic and let the "turnover" rest for 15 minutes or so. (If you are doing this in the heat of summer, let the dough rest in the refrigerator.)

Remove the plastic. Lightly flour the top of the "turnover". Lift the "turnover" one half at a time and flour underneath it. Gently press the dough down with your fingers. Use a rolling pin to roll the dough first one direction and then the other, flouring only as needed, until it is a rectangle roughly 12 x 18 inches. When the dough sticks to the rolling surface, scrape half of it off and flop it over onto the other half and reflour underneath it. **(C)** Repeat for the other half. If the butter squeezes out, scrape it up and put it back onto the dough and dab it with a bit of extra flour. Try to use only as much flour as you need; too much additional flour will affect the dough's quality.

A

B

Délice

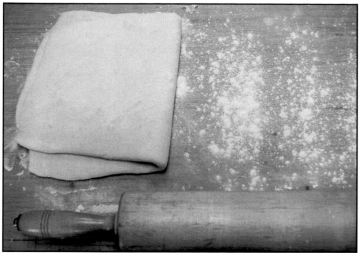

C

Once you have created the rectangle, use a dry pastry brush to brush any excess flour from the top surface. Fold the dough into three layers by first grasping one of the short ends and pulling it so that the third of that end of the dough lies over the middle one-third of the dough. Gently push or pull the dough to make the corners meet the edges of the dough that is underneath. Brush any excess flour off the surface of the dough. Fold the remaining third of the dough onto the top of the other two layers. Gently push or pull the dough to make the corners all meet. Turn the dough one quarter turn and roll it into another 12 x 18 inch rectangle. Repeat the folding process. Cover the dough with plastic and let it rest for 15 minutes or more.

Remove the plastic. Lightly flour the top of the dough and underneath the dough and roll it into another 12 x 18 inch rectangle. Repeat the 1/3rd folding process. Turn the dough one quarter turn and roll it into a rectangle one last time. Repeat the folding process. In total you should have rolled and folded the dough 4 times with a rest between each set of 2 rollings.

Place the dough into a parchment lined pan or dish and cover it with plastic. Refrigerate it for an hour or more before using it for whichever recipe it was intended. Do not refrigerate puffpastry for more than a day; it turns gray. Freeze it, wrapped tightly with plastic, for up to a couple of months.* Defrost puffpastry by placing it into the refrigerator the night before or letting it sit at room temperature for a couple of hours before it is needed. Do not microwave it! If it gets too soft and butter escapes when it is rolled, chill it briefly.

Walter's note: For faster defrosting, store the dough in layers ¼ inch thick with 2 sheets of wax paper or parchment between each one.

BUTTERFLIES

Also known as elephant ears, palmier, pig's ears, or papillon, this was our number one selling pastry. We had customers that preferred them very lightly baked, and others that liked the darker ones, when the sugar has truly caramelized. We even had one gentleman who we often gifted with the ones that we considered burnt beyond all hope.

Depending on how you choose to fold the puffpastry, the result can be large butterflies roughly the size of the ones we sold or much smaller ones. Ideally butterflies should be eaten shortly after coming out of the oven, but they can be frozen at any point in the process, as long as they are hot when you glaze them. One warning: Do not refrigerate the puffpastry once it has been rolled in the sugar; freeze or bake it.

Makes 12-18 butterflies.

Prepare puffpastry (page 48) the day before or several hours ahead (or purchase it from the freezer section at the grocery store.)

1 cup powdered sugar
1 tablespoon + 2 teaspoons hot water
¾ cup sugar
3 tablespoons apricot jam or syrup (peach will work)

If using purchased puffpastry, defrost it according to the directions.

Preheat oven all the way to 400°.

Prepare and then set aside a plain sugar glaze by mixing together the powdered sugar and the hot water. Line at least one baking sheet with parchment paper. Place the sugar in a bowl, readily accessible.

Sprinkle a rolling surface liberally with the sugar, place homemade puffpastry on it and liberally sprinkle the top with sugar. Roll the puffpastry out to a rectangle roughly 12 x 20 inches, sprinkling periodically with sugar. If using purchased puffpastry sheets, sprinkle a rolling surface liberally with sugar and unfold two sheets. Create one large sheet by brushing water or eggwash onto a half inch of one edge of one sheet and then placing an edge of the second sheet overlapping the

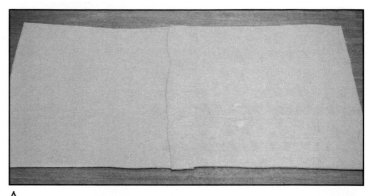

A

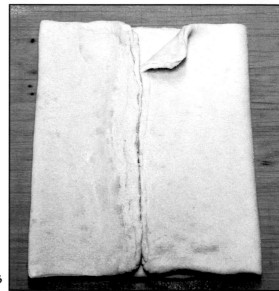

B

water or eggwash. Press the layered seam with your fingers or a rolling pin. **(A)** Sprinkle the entire dough with sugar, roll it enough to press the sugar into the surface. Gently turn it over and sprinkle with more sugar. Roll the seam out to the same thickness as the surrounding puffpastry.

Whether using homemade or purchased puffpastry, lift one of the short ends over the middle third of the dough. Lift the opposite end over the top of the two layers to create three layers. Turn the dough a quarter turn. Lift each end in turn in order to dust the underneath with more sugar. Dust the top with more sugar. Roll the dough out to the same thickness it was before folding it, being sure to maintain a rectangle approximately twice as long as it is wide. Ideally, you should have used at least ½ cup of the sugar.

Délice

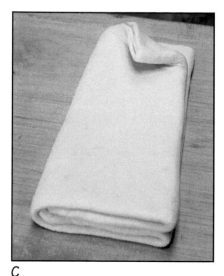

C

Large butterflies:

To create a centerline, fold one short end over to meet the other edge, then open it back up. Fold each short end in to the centerline. **(B)** Use a pastry brush or your fingers to brush a stripe of water the length of one folded side (to act as glue). Folding at the centerline, lift one side up over the other. **(C)** Using a French style knife, cut across the face of the "roll", creating 3/8 – 1/2 inch slices. **(D)** The slices can be baked or frozen. Any slices that cannot be baked right away should be frozen, even if it is only for the time needed to wait for oven space. To freeze, place into an airtight container with wax or parchment paper between layers.

D

To bake the butterflies, place the slices (freshly cut or frozen) onto a parchment lined baking sheet in a way that they can expand sideways. If using homemade puffpastry, bake for 15 minutes at 400°, then turn the oven down to 300° and carefully turn the tray around in the oven to try to prevent uneven baking. Bake at the lower temperature for 10-20 minutes or until the butterflies are brown not just on the edges, but in places across the middle. If using purchased puffpastry, bake at 400° for 15 minutes, but cut the baking time at 300° to 5-7 minutes.

Small butterflies:

Follow all the rolling directions for the large butterflies, except when folding them into their final "roll", use the long edges instead of the short edges. Cut the slices approximately 3/8 inch thick. For homemade puffpastry, bake at 400° for 10 minutes, then at 300° for an additional 25-40 minutes (15-20 minutes if using purchased puffpastry) or until the butterflies are brown not just on the edges, but in places across the middle.

Glazing hot butterflies:

Measure the apricot jam or syrup into a microwave-safe cup or small bowl or into a small saucepan. If using jam, thin it by adding a few drops of water to it. Set it aside. Have a pastry brush handy. Just before the butterflies are about to come out of the oven, heat the apricot in a microwave for 15-20 seconds or bring it just to a boil in a small saucepan on the stove. The moment the butterflies are removed from the oven, quickly brush them thinly with the hot apricot jam or syrup and then with the sugar glaze. **(E)**

E

BOWTIES

Bowties are twisted layers of puffpastry with almond and cinnamon. Whenever we baked these, the smell would seep into the ventilation system and permeate the entire building. We would get "complaints" about the tempting aroma from the girls in the offices upstairs. We even had customers that would recognize the aroma upon walking in and request one be glazed hot out of the oven for them.

Like the butterflies, these can be frozen at any point in the process, as long as they are hot when you glaze them. This is actually two recipes; one for using purchased puffpastry and one for using homemade puffpastry. Commercially produced puffpastry behaves a bit differently in the oven. As a result, the alternative "cookie" shape is not a viable option with the purchased version.

Using homemade puffpastry:
Makes 22 bowties.

Prepare puffpastry (page 48) the day before or several hours ahead.

1-¼ cups almond meal or flour (see Glossary)
¾ cup + 1 tablespoon sugar
4 tablespoons milk
A skimpy ¼ teaspoon vanilla
2 teaspoons ground cinnamon
3 tablespoons apricot jam or syrup
1 cup powdered sugar
1 tablespoon + 2 teaspoons hot water

If you have not used roasted almonds to make your own almond meal, preheat oven or toaster oven to 350°. In a metal baking pan, roast the almond meal until it just begins to color around the edges (approximately 5-8 minutes). Stir the almond meal and continue to roast an additional 2 minutes. (Skip this roasting step if roasted almonds were used to make the almond meal.) Let the roasted almond meal cool to room temperature.

In a bowl, use a sturdy spoon to mix together the roasted almond meal, the sugar and 3 tablespoons of the milk. Add additional milk ½ teaspoon at a time only until the whole is a thick paste. Into the almond paste, mix the vanilla and the ground cinnamon. Set aside.

Preheat oven all the way to 400°.

Line at least one baking sheet with parchment paper. On a lightly floured surface, roll the puffpastry into a 15 x 22 inch rectangle. Leave approximately 4-½ inches at one of the short ends clear and gently spread the almond paste across the remainder of the rectangle. Be sure to spread it all the way out to the edges. Cut the rectangle into 5 roughly equal "strips", the clear portion being one of the five. Carefully stack the four portions with almond paste such that they are one on top of each other, four deep. Turn the clear portion of puffpastry over and use it as the top of the stack.

Use a French style knife to cut ½ inch thick slices from one short end of the stack. If the stack "squishes" when cut, place it onto a tray and refrigerate it for an hour. Carefully twist each slice in the middle and place them onto the parchment lined baking sheet, allowing plenty of room for them to expand sideways. Any bowties that cannot be baked immediately should be cut, twisted, frozen and then baked straight from the freezer. Do not refrigerate or leave them at room temperature.

Bake at 400° for 10 minutes, then turn the oven down to 300° and continue to bake for 25-35 minutes or until the puffpastry is baked toward the centers of the twist. While the bowties bake, prepare a plain sugar glaze by mixing the powdered sugar and the hot water. Set it aside. Measure the apricot jam or syrup into a microwave-safe cup or bowl or into a small saucepan. If using jam, thin it by adding a few drops of water to it. Set it aside. Have a pastry brush handy. Just before the bowties are about to come out of the oven, heat the apricot in a microwave for 15-20 seconds or bring it just to a boil in a small saucepan on the stove. Immediately after the bowties come out of the oven, brush each one with the warmed apricot and then with the sugar glaze.

Simpler configuration ("Pacman"-shaped cookies):

Preheat oven all the way to 400°.

On a lightly floured surface, roll homemade puffpastry into a 15 x 22 inch rectangle. Brush one inch of one long edge with eggwash (see Glossary) or water. Gently spread the almond paste over the remainder of the rectangle, being sure to spread it all the way out to the short edges. Beginning with the unbrushed long edge, roll the rectangle toward the brushed edge to create a long "log" roll. Cut ½ inch slices and place on a parchment lined baking sheet. Use a small knife to cut each swirl once to the center to allow the puffpastry room to expand. Bake as you would bowties, cutting the time at 300° back by 5-10 minutes. Glaze the same as bowties.

Using purchased puffpastry sheets:
Makes 15 bowties.

2 sheets puffpastry
1 cup almond meal or flour (see Glossary)
²⁄₃ cup sugar
3 tablespoons milk
⅛ teaspoon vanilla
1-½ teaspoons ground cinnamon
3 tablespoons apricot jam
1 cup powdered sugar
1 tablespoon + 2 teaspoons hot water

If you have not used roasted almonds to make your own almond meal, preheat oven or toaster oven to 350°. In a metal baking pan, roast the almond meal until it just begins to color around the edges (approximately 5-8 minutes). Stir the almond meal and continue to roast an additional 2 minutes. (Skip this roasting step if roasted almonds were used to make the almond meal.) Let the roasted almond meal cool to room temperature.

In a bowl, use a sturdy spoon to mix together the roasted almond meal, the sugar and 2-½ tablespoons of the milk. Add additional milk ½ teaspoon at a time only until the whole is a thick paste. Into the almond paste, mix the vanilla and the ground cinnamon. Set aside.

Preheat oven all the way to 400°.

Line at least one baking sheet with parchment paper. Unfold two 10 x 10 inch pastry sheets. Cut one of them in half. Spread the almond paste on one of the resulting halves AND the entire second sheet, being sure to spread it all the way out to the edges. Now cut the second sheet in half also. You should have three "strips" with almond paste on them and one without. Carefully stack the three portions with almond paste such that they are one on top of each other, three deep. Turn the clear strip over and use it as the top of the stack.

Use a French style knife to cut ½ inch thick slices from one short end of the stack. If the stack "squishes" when cut, place it onto a tray and refrigerate it for an hour. Carefully twist each slice in the middle and place them onto the parchment lined baking sheet, allowing plenty of room for them to expand sideways. Any bowties that cannot be baked immediately should be cut, twisted, frozen and then baked straight from the freezer. Do not refrigerate or leave them at room temperature.

Bake at 400° for 10 minutes, then turn the oven down to 300° and continue to bake for 6-10 minutes or until the puffpastry is baked toward the centers of the twist. While the bowties bake, prepare a plain sugar glaze by mixing the powdered sugar and the hot water. Set it aside. Measure the apricot jam or syrup into a microwave-safe cup or bowl or into a small saucepan. If using jam, thin it by adding a few drops of water to it. Set it aside. Have a pastry brush handy. Just before the bowties are about to come out of the oven, heat the apricot in a microwave for 15-20 seconds or bring it just to a boil in a small saucepan on the stove. Immediately after the bowties come out of the oven, brush each one with the warmed apricot and then with the sugar glaze.

APPLE STRUDEL

The apple strudel was one of the elite pastries that we baked every single morning. We prepared the filling in huge batches using nearly 40 pounds of frozen sliced apples, pressed it into 3 full-sized sheet trays, and froze them before cutting them to size. We would then wrap the cut portions in the puffpastry and freeze them to bake as needed. Since freezing the filling is not truly necessary at home, I have offered directions for skipping the freezer. Apple strudel is delicious either as an after-dinner dessert served with sweetened whip cream or cinnamon ice cream or try it for breakfast.

Makes 2 apple strudels.

Prepare puffpastry (page 48) the day before or several hours ahead (or purchase it from the freezer section at the grocery store.)

Prepare the Apricot Sugar Glaze recipe (page 42) and set aside or refrigerate.

Prepare an eggwash (see Glossary) and set aside.

4 cups water
2 teaspoons lemon juice
4 large granny smith apples (5-½ - 6 cups sliced)
6 tablespoons sugar
2 teaspoons flour
1-¼ teaspoons ground cinnamon
a small grating of lemon zest or a teaspoon of
   lemon juice
3 tablespoons chopped walnuts
3 tablespoons raisins
1 tablespoon sliced, roasted almonds (optional)

The apple filling:

Pour the water and lemon juice into a large bowl. Peel, core and thinly slice the apples, putting them into the lemon water as you slice them. When done, drain the lemon water away. To the apple slices, add the remaining ingredients except for the almonds. Stir or toss until the apples are evenly coated.

If you wish to freeze the filling to wrap in puffpastry later, split the apple mixture between two 9 x 5 inch loaf pans and press it down. Cover each with plastic wrap

and freeze. They can remain frozen for several weeks. If you need your pans for other uses in the meantime, once the apple is frozen hard, take it out and keep it in the freezer well wrapped in plastic. (If the apples are stubborn about coming out of the pan, gently heat the bottom of the pan by dipping it in hot water very briefly.)

The filling and the puffpastry come together:

If you intend to bake the strudel, preheat the oven to 400°.

If your "optional" almonds aren't roasted, put them into a metal loaf or pie pan and bake them for 3-4 minutes or until they just begin to brown. Set them aside.

If using homemade puffpastry, roll the puffpastry out to a rectangle 15 x 25 inches. Cut it in half across the short width to create two sheets. If using purchased puffpastry sheets, roll two sheets of 10 x 10 inch puffpastry until they are an additional inch square. If the apple filling is fresh, divide it between the two puffpastry sheets, placing it on half of each piece and leaving an inch of puffpastry showing on each end and down the edge. **(A)** If the apple filling is frozen, simply place one of the apple fillings onto each of the puffpastry sheets, an inch from one of the long edges.

A

APPLE STRUDEL cont.

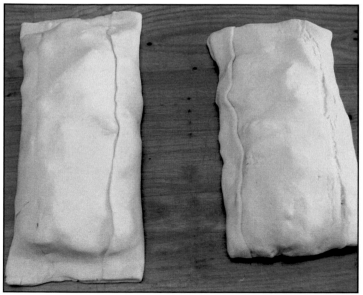

B

Brush eggwash onto the inch of exposed puffpastry edge and an inch at each end of where the apple is. Lift the other edge over the apples just until it covers the apples. Fold the eggwashed edge up over the edge that you just covered the apples with and gently press it down. Use the side of your hand to press the puffpastry down just where the filling ends to seal it in. If there is more than an inch and a half of puffpastry at each end, cut away any excess.* Fold the puffpastry ends up underneath. **(B)** Brush the top of the puffpastry with eggwash and use the tip of a knife to poke two or three vent holes in the top. **(C)** Place the strudels on a rimmed baking sheet to either freeze or bake, or do one of each.

Baking:

Preheat oven all the way to 400°.

Bake freshly wrapped strudel for 40 minutes or until the puffpastry is nicely brown. If the strudel is frozen, bake an additional 10 minutes, or more if needed. Once out of the oven, brush the top generously with the glaze and sprinkle the roasted almonds into the warm glaze. Serve warm or freeze for future use.

*Cynthia's note: I can't stand to see hard work go to waste. Brush any leftover puffpastry with melted butter and sprinkle with cinnamon and sugar, cut into smaller pieces if necessary and roll them up. Bake them in a 400° oven until brown.

C

Délice _____

NAPOLEANS

Napoleans are vanilla Custard Cream layered between flaky Puffpastry with either a pretty pink glaze on top or a simple dusting of powdered sugar. These were not among the regular pastries in the showcase, because Walter insisted that they be eaten the same day that they were prepared. Therefore they were a very special treat when we expected to be exceptionally busy or on special occasions. According to my husband's co-workers, though, Napoleans are still absolutely delectable even after being refrigerated overnight.

This is actually 2 recipes; one using homemade Puffpastry and one using the purchased version.

Makes 14 Napoleans.

Prepare puffpastry (page 48) the day before or several hours ahead (or purchase it from the freezer section at the grocery store.)

Assemble ingredients for Custard Cream recipe (page 43).

Icing:
¾ cup powdered sugar
1 tablespoon hot water
1 drop red food color

Preheat oven all the way to 400°.

Using Purchased Puffpastry:
Defrost according to the directions. Carefully unfold two 10 x 10 inch sheets of puffpastry. Use a fork (or two forks if you wish to use both hands) to thoroughly perforate (poke holes in) the puffpastry, being sure to go all the way out to the edges. **(A)** Turn each sheet over and repeat the perforation on the other side.

A

B

Bake each sheet on a parchment lined baking sheet for 10 minutes at 400°; then, without opening the oven door, turn the temperature down to 375°. Bake the puffpastry for an additional 10 minutes before checking it and gently turning the tray around to assure even browning. Bake for 3-6 minutes more or until it is completely baked and flaky and has browned. Take the tray from the oven and very, very carefully turn the pastry over and place it back into the oven for five minutes to crisp the "bottom". Should the pastry puff a bit, let it cool a minute or two, but while it is still warm, very gently press it down. Let cool to room temperature. While it is cooling, prepare the custard cream or once the pastry is cool, freeze it and layer it at a later time.

Prepare the custard cream according to the recipe and let it cool to a temperature that will not burn your fingers while you are working with it.

To create a pastry with 3 layers of puffpastry and two layers of custard cream, cut 1/3rd of each baked puffpastry sheet away and set these two narrow pieces to one side. Spread ½ of the custard cream over one of the two larger sheets of puffpastry. Carefully place the other large sheet over this and spread the remaining custard cream on the top of it. Place the two narrow sheets side by side on top of the cream.

continued on next page...

Prepare the icing by using a wire whip to stir the ingredients together in a bowl, then placing the bowl over a small saucepan of hot water (double boiler) for 5 minutes. Spread the icing over the two narrow sheets of puffpastry. Use a serrated knife in a sawing action to, first, cut the layers lengthwise between the two narrow puffpastry sheets, then cut across the stack to create rectangles. If not using icing, cut the Napoleans, then, just before serving them, dust with powdered sugar.

Using Homemade Puffpastry:

Cut the puffpastry in half across the short width. Freeze one half for future use. Roll the remaining half out into a rectangle approximately 11 x 15 inches. Use a fork (or two forks if using both hands) to perforate (poke lots of holes in) the puffpastry, being sure to go all the way out to the edges. **(B)**

Bake at 400° for 5 minutes, then, without opening the oven door turn the oven down to 375° and bake for another 20-25 minutes. Take the tray from the oven and very, very carefully turn the pastry over and bake for 4-5 minutes to crisp the "bottom". Let the baked puffpastry cool to room temperature. While it is cooling, prepare the custard cream or once the pastry is cool, freeze it and layer it at a later time.

Prepare the custard cream according to the recipe and let it cool to a temperature that will not burn your fingers while you are working with it.

Cut the baked puffpastry into 3 equal portions. **(C)** Spread ½ of the custard cream over one of the three portions. **(D)** Carefully place one of the other portions on top of the cream. Spread the remaining custard cream over this. **(E)** Place the final portion on the top. **(F)**

Prepare the icing by stirring the ingredients together in a bowl, then placing the bowl over a small saucepan of hot water (double boiler) for 5 minutes. Spread the icing over the top sheet of puffpastry. (**G**) Use a serrated knife in a sawing action to, first, cut the layers in half lengthwise, then cut across the stack to create rectangles. If not using icing, cut the Napoleans, then, just before serving them, dust with powdered sugar.

C

D

E

F

G

CHERRY CREAM CHEESE "PIZZA" PIE

We called this torte "pizza" because of its pizza-like appearance. Many of the young customers that came across the street from the high school for lunch simply asked for a slice of the "cherry thing".

We produced thirty or more cherry "pizzas" at a time and kept them frozen, ready to bake. Each morning we would bake two or three. We offered the cherry "pie" by the slice or frozen whole, already baked and glazed. We recommended letting the whole frozen ones defrost at room temperature or popping them back into a 400° oven just until the glaze began to bubble. These tortes can be the perfect thing to make ahead and keep frozen for an impromptu dessert or breakfast treat.

Makes 2 "pizzas".

Prepare puffpastry (page 48) the day before or several hours ahead (or purchase it from the freezer section at the grocery store.)

Prepare the Apricot Sugar Glaze recipe (page 42) and refrigerate.

4 teaspoons minute tapioca
9 tablespoons + 2-½ teaspoons sugar, divided
3 tablespoons corn starch, divided
7 tablespoons water, divided
1 can (14-½ ounce) tart pitted cherries
8 ounces regular cream cheese
1 egg

If using homemade puffpastry, roll it out into a rectangle approximately ¼ inch thick. If using purchased puffpastry, defrost it according to the directions and unfold it. Use an 8 or 9 inch cake pan to sit on the puffpastry as a pattern. Use a jagger (see Glossary), a rotary pizza cutter, or a knife, to cut around the bottom of the cake pan to create two 8 or 9 inch puffpastry circles. Leaving a half-inch around the edge of each circle untouched, use a fork to perforate the puffpastry repeatedly. This prevents the pastry from puffing in the middle and having the cherry layer run off.

Place the circles onto a couple of cardboard cake circles or a parchment lined baking sheet. Wrap with plastic and freeze. Small freezer space? Stack the puffpastry circles with parchment or wax paper in between them.

These puffpastry bottoms can be made a week or two ahead and kept in the freezer.

Measure the tapioca and 4 teaspoons of the sugar into a small bowl and stir them together. Set them aside. In another small bowl, mix together 2 tablespoons of the corn starch and 2 tablespoons of cold water. Set them aside also. In a medium-sized saucepan, over medium heat, bring the cherries, 5 tablespoons of sugar and 5 tablespoons of water to a boil. Add the tapioca/sugar, stirring only enough to mix the ingredients in. Too much stirring breaks the cherries. Simmer 5 minutes. Gently add and stir in the diluted corn starch. Stirring once or twice, simmer a minute or two and remove from heat. Let cool to room temperature. In a hurry? Spread the cherry mixture out in an edged baking sheet; it will cool quicker.

Take the puffpastry circles out of the freezer and divide the cherry mixture between them. Keeping the cherry mixture an inch or so from the edge, use a spatula to spread the mixture to an even thickness. Freeze uncovered until the cherries begin to stiffen (1-½ - 2 hours, or if you have the time, overnight).

While the cherries set up, prepare the cream cheese topping by creaming together the cream cheese, 3-½ tablespoons of sugar, 1 tablespoon of corn starch and ½ of an egg (open the egg into a small bowl, stir it with a fork and then measure 1-½ tablespoons of it). The resulting cream cheese mixture can be covered and refrigerated until needed.

Once the cherries have stiffened, divide the cream cheese mixture between the two circles and use a spatula to spread it over the cherries, being sure to let the cherries show around the edges.

Preheat oven all the way to 400°.

Take the apricot sugar glaze out of the refrigerator and let it sit at room temperature. Have a pastry brush handy. Place one or both "pizza(s)" on a metal baking sheet with a rim. Bake for 30 minutes or until the cream cheese begins to brown around the edges and a bit across the top. Gently brush the entire surface with the glaze immediately after removal from the oven. Serve warm or at room temperature.

Délice

Chocolate Pastries

The Faas family enjoying lunch

SARAH BERNHARDTS

Born Henriette Rosine Bernard, the French stage actress and courtesan Sarah Bernhardt was renowned as "The Divine Sarah". Famous across Europe and even in the U.S., her career spanned the turn of the century into the silent movie era, even after her right leg was amputated in 1915.

Why these little mountains of chocolate were named after the French actress seems to be lost in the mists of time. Our frequent high school-aged customers generally referred to them as Dolly Partons. Sarah Bernhardt looked nothing like Dolly Parton. Perhaps Ms. Bernhardt just really liked chocolate.

This recipe makes approximately 20 Sarahs, but, creating Sarahs falls into the cake and ice cream syndrome. You are likely to end up with either leftover whipped canache or leftover meringues. The meringue recipe can be affected by such nebulous factors as the eggs' temperatures or the ambient humidity, and the volume to which the canache eventually whips up to is equally unpredictable. Someone will likely be willing to eat whatever is leftover.

Prepare Baked Meringues with Almond (page 83) (ahead of time is best).

When piping the whipped meringue onto a parchment lined baking sheet, create small rounds roughly the size of a quarter or fifty-cent piece. Do NOT sprinkle them with almond flour. Gently press down any pointy tips that exist, as this will make piping the chocolate on top of them easier. Do not refrigerate the meringues. If you make them ahead, let them cool to room temperature, then roll them up in the parchment paper and put them into a plastic bag and leave them at room temperature (up to a couple of days).

Prepare Canache (page 44) and let cool to room temperature, then chill for an hour or overnight. Do not whip yet.

Chocolate coating:
10-12 ounces milk chocolate coating or milk chocolate
1 teaspoon vegetable oil

Place the meringues onto a tray. Whip the canache according to the recipe, allowing time for several temperature corrections if necessary. Immediately put the whipped chocolate into a pastry bag or plastic sandwich bag with a half-inch cut made across one corner. Pipe the whipped canache onto each meringue, starting strong, then letting off and pulling the bag straight up. **(A)** Ideally each one should look something like a big Hershey's® kiss. **(B)** Put them in the freezer until hard (10-20 minutes).

A

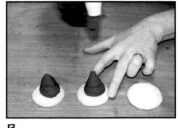

B

Melt the milk chocolate by using a double-boiler over low-medium heat or microwaving it, then stirring it, in 5-10 second intervals. Do not overheat it, just melt it. Stir the vegetable oil into the chocolate. Pour a portion of the chocolate into something that is going to be deep enough to dip each Sarah into, yet wide enough at the top for you to hold onto the Sarah as you are dipping it. Take the Sarahs from the freezer and let them sit at room temperature for 2-3 minutes. Dip each Sarah all the way to the bottom of the meringue, pull it out of the chocolate so that just the tip is still dipped. **(C)** Shake it a bit to allow gravity to pull any excess chocolate back into the container. Place the Sarah back onto the tray. You may have to add more melted chocolate as the level drops. If the chocolate does not harden at room temperature, freeze or refrigerate the Sarahs for a few minutes.

C

Keep cool. To store, freeze in an airtight container.

FLORENTINES

We described the Florentines to our customers as almond toffee backed with milk chocolate. We sold individual bars or 4 ounce containers full of bite-size squares that we called "nibblers". As one of our very best selling pastries, the Florentines truly showed off Walter's classical training in candy making. They take time, but are well worth every minute. Fill little decorative bags or boxes as gifts.

Makes 32-36 bars or 8 cups of nibblers.

2-½ cups raw sliced almonds
¾ cup sugar
3-½ tablespoons honey
3-½ tablespoons light corn syrup
¼ cup half and half
1-⅓ tablespoon butter, divided
1 tablespoon margarine
8 ounces milk chocolate or milk chocolate coating
½ teaspoon vegetable oil

Measure the almonds and set them aside. Measure the sugar and place it into a shallow bowl and create a depression in the center by pushing the sugar up the edges of the bowl, being sure not to leave any 'holes'. Measure the honey and scrape it into the depression made in the sugar, trying not to let it actually touch the bowl. Measure the corn syrup and add it gently to the depression as well. Ideally, the sugar will keep the gooey corn syrup and honey from sticking to the bowl when you need to add them to the melted butter. Set the sugar/honey/corn syrup aside. Measure the half and half and set it aside as well.

A brief word of caution: boiling sugar can really burn, so treat it with respect. Choose a heavy saucepan large enough that all the ingredients can be stirred in it. On medium heat, melt 1 tablespoon of the butter and the margarine. Use a wire whip to stir the half and half and the sugar/honey/corn syrup into the saucepan. Still on medium heat, slowly bring it all to a boil, stirring often. Stirring almost constantly, boil for 4 minutes. It can burn, so do not walk too far away from it. Remove the mixture from the heat. Use a sturdy spoon to stir the almonds into the mixture. Scrape the coated almonds

into a 9 x 5 inch loaf pan or a 9 x 9 inch baking pan. Use a spatula to press the contents down. Let the coated almonds cool to room temperature.

Go on to the baking phase, or wrap the loaf or baking pan with plastic and refrigerate it for up to several days. The coated almonds can even be frozen for several weeks. It is easiest to let them reach room temperature again before continuing.

Preheat oven to 350°.

Cut a piece of parchment to fit an 11 x 17 inch rimmed baking sheet. Set it aside. Melt ⅓ tablespoon of butter. Brush the melted butter in an inch wide band next to the rim of the baking sheet. Place the parchment down and smooth it. The butter should keep the candy-like almonds from oozing underneath the parchment.

Cut the coated almonds into small strips and, if soft enough, flatten them between your fingers. Place them haphazardly, in a single layer, onto the parchment lined baking sheet. Put the sheet into the oven. After 10 minutes, carefully turn the sheet around and let the florentines bake for another 2-5 minutes. The toffee will become bubbly and as the sugar caramelizes it will brown. Take the toffee out of the oven when the dark brown color has spread to more than half of the tray. For best results you may have to let the portions near the edges of the pan get too dark, but they can be cut away later.

Once you have removed the toffee from the oven, let it sit just long enough for the bubbles to subside. Do not let it cool completely before cutting, since it will become very brittle. Use a French style knife or a dough cutter to create either rectangular or bite-size seams in the warm toffee. There is no need to cut all the way through, but simply create a seam. Once cooled to room temperature, the toffee should break at the seams.

continued on next page...

Délice _____

If you have chosen to make individual bars, carefully separate the toffee pieces at the seams and place them onto a parchment or wax paper lined tray or sheet. Before coating them with chocolate, be sure that the florentines are room temperature (or warmer); if cold, the chocolate will not stick.

Melt the milk chocolate by using a double-boiler over low-medium heat or microwaving it, then stirring it, in 5-10 second intervals. Stir the vegetable oil into the chocolate. For bars, use a metal spatula to spread melted milk chocolate onto the back of each florentine. Use the edge of the spatula to create a decorative lined effect in the chocolate. Freeze or refrigerate the florentines momentarily to harden the chocolate.

To chocolate coat "nibblers", first use a knife or similar tool to loosen the parchment from the baking sheet. Place another baking sheet or a tray tightly over the baking sheet of florentines. Turn the whole assembly over. Slide the upside down florentines onto a countertop, large cutting board or back onto one of the baking sheets. Remove the parchment. Spoon all of the melted chocolate out onto the bottom of the florentines and crudely spread it as best you can. (Dark German words always seemed to help Walter accomplish this challenging task.) Freeze or refrigerate briefly to harden the chocolate.

Serve at room temperature or chilled for a less chewy experience. Florentines can be frozen or refrigerated for considerable periods if kept in airtight bags or containers.

Walter, the PR guy

Délice

RUMBALLS

We had several customers that were passionate about the Rumballs. Although we kept a bottle of rum flavoring on the shelf to appease the health inspector, the truth is that we never used it. Only the real thing will do. Walter never measured the amount of rum, he just poured, so I have given you the choice of how potent you prefer them to be. We hand rolled every single Rumball. The sensation of having your fingers coated with chocolate can be quite amusing.

Makes 20-24 rumballs.

Prepare Canache (page 44) and let cool to room temperature, then chill for an hour or overnight.

2 or 3 tablespoons gold (dark) rum
8 ounces milk chocolate coating or milk chocolate

Whip the canache according to the recipe, allowing time for several temperature corrections if necessary. Use a hand held wire whip to stir the rum into the canache. Choose a baking sheet or other flat surface that will fit into your freezer. Line it with parchment paper. Use a pastry bag without a tip in it or a plastic sandwich bag with a half inch cut made across one corner, to create quarter or fifty-cent size dollops of the canache on the parchment. **(A)** Put the sheet into the freezer uncovered, until the dollops are hard (10-20 minutes).

B

Melt the chocolate by using a double-boiler over low-medium heat or microwaving it, then stirring it, in 5-10 second intervals. Take the rum/canache dollops from the freezer and let them sit at room temperature for 2-3 minutes. Pick up one piece of the canache in each hand. Dip the flat side of one of them into the milk chocolate and press them together. Sit this "ball" back onto the parchment and repeat the process for the remaining halves. **(B)** Now pick up the first ball, dip it generously into the milk chocolate and roll it around between the fingers of both hands. Place it back onto the parchment and repeat the process for each ball. After each one has one coat of chocolate, place the tray into the refrigerator for 1-2 minutes, just long enough for the chocolate to harden. Repeat the coating process a second time for each ball. Do not lick your fingers until all of them are rolled twice. Place the balls, uncovered, into the freezer or refrigerator for several minutes until the chocolate hardens.

Serve chilled. Store in an airtight container in the freezer.

A

PEPPERMINT SQUARES

In my mind the name for these is a misnomer, because really, it's all about the chocolate. Of course, that's coming from a lifetime chocoholic. We always used milk chocolate when layering these, but if you prefer dark chocolate, use it instead of the milk chocolate. When testing recipes for this book, pastry samples often went out to friends, the family's co-workers and in some special instances, former customers that I knew had particular favorites, but the Peppermint Squares never left the house.

Makes 20 squares.

Prepare Canache (page 44) and let cool to room temperature, then chill for an hour or overnight.

1 teaspoon peppermint extract
9 ounces milk chocolate or milk chocolate coating
   (1-½ cups chocolate chips)

Line a baking sheet with parchment paper. It is helpful to tape the paper down with masking tape. Whip the canache according to the recipe, allowing time for several temperature corrections if necessary. Whip the peppermint extract into the canache. Onto the parchment paper, spread the peppermint canache into a 9 x 12 inch rectangle (approximately 1/4 - 3/8 inch thick). Freeze until solid (10-15 minutes).

Melt the milk chocolate by using a double-boiler over low-medium heat or microwaving it, then stirring it, in 5-10 second intervals. Remove the peppermint canache from the freezer and let it sit at room temperature for 2-3 minutes. Spread half of the milk chocolate over the canache, working quickly as the warm chocolate will tend to melt the canache. Place uncovered into the refrigerator for 3-4 minutes to harden. Place a second sheet of parchment over the chocolate rectangle and very carefully turn it over. Peel the parchment off of the canache and coat it with the remaining milk chocolate. Place back into the refrigerator for another 3-4 minutes to harden.

Cut squares using a knife that has been warmed in hot water and wiped dry. This process may have to be repeated several times to cut the entire rectangle. (If you accidentally forget it in the refrigerator and it gets really hard, let it sit at room temperature for 5-10 minutes before trying to cut it.) The squares are easier to handle if frozen briefly. Pick them up by the edges to avoid leaving fingerprints in the milk chocolate.

PALETTE

This is the simplest pastry we did. If you purchase the almonds already roasted (which is a shortcut we never used), you are most of the way there. Yet, your family and friends will be so impressed with the results. We always used white chocolate, but I don't see any reason not to try your favorite milk or dark chocolate.

Makes 9-11 (2-½ inch) circles.

²/₃ cup sliced, roasted almonds (see Roasted Almonds, page 42)
8 ounces white chocolate or white chocolate coating
   (1-¼ cup chocolate chips)

Roast the sliced almonds, if needed. Line a baking sheet with parchment. If using already roasted almonds, be sure that they are room temperature. (Nuts should be stored in the freezer.) Place the chocolate, chopped or broken into small pieces (if not using chips), into a double boiler. Melt the chocolate over low to medium heat. Remove from heat and wipe the moisture from the bottom of the bowl or pan to prevent accidentally dripping water onto the palette. Stir the roasted almonds into the melted chocolate. Use a tablespoon to drop a portion of the mixture onto the parchment lined sheet. Use the back of the spoon to spread it into a 2-½ inch circle. Repeat the process for all of the mixture. Refrigerate 10 minutes to harden the chocolate.

Serve chilled. Store in an airtight container or plastic bag in the freezer or refrigerator.

Délice

CHOCOLATE SQUARES

A thick layer of chocolate whipped with butter and milk is sandwiched between two almond wafers, then topped with decorative milk chocolate. Rich, but not too sweet, these will satisfy any chocolate craving.

Makes 24 squares.

Prepare Viennese Wafer Dough (page 45) and refrigerate several hours or overnight.

Prepare Canache (page 44) and let cool to room temperature, then chill for an hour or overnight. Do not whip yet.

2 ounces milk chocolate or milk chocolate coating

Preheat oven to 300°.

Place baking rack high up in the oven. Have handy an 11 x 17 inch rimmed baking sheet or a cookie sheet. Prepare a rolling surface by dusting it with flour. Roll the Viennese wafer dough out into a large rectangle, approximately 3/8ths inch thick. Dust the top of the dough and carefully roll it around your rolling pin. Unroll the dough very gently over the baking sheet. Use your fingers to press the dough together wherever it may have torn. Use a knife or dough cutter to cut the dough to fit the bottom of the rimmed baking sheet, or if using a cookie sheet, trim the edges to create a neat rectangle. Measure or "eyeball" the center of the dough and cut it in half. Leave one half whole. Cut the other half into squares the size you wish the final pastries to be.

Bake for 25-30 minutes, turning the tray around once, until the edges begin to brown. Should the dough begin to "bubble", use a knife or toothpick inserted into the bubble to let the steam out. Let cool to room temperature. If you choose to bake the squares ahead and freeze or refrigerate them, heat them briefly in a 200° oven before layering them. If the wafer dough is too cold the layers will not stick together.

Whip the canache according to the recipe, allowing time for several temperature corrections if necessary. Spread all of the whipped canache over the 'whole' half of baked Viennese Wafer Dough. **(A)** Place the squares over the canache. Press them gently onto the canache. **(B)**

Melt the milk chocolate by using a double-boiler over low-medium heat or microwaving it, then stirring it, in 5-10 second intervals. Working quickly, spread the milk chocolate thinly over the rectangles. Before the chocolate hardens, repeatedly pull a fork diagonally across the top and then repeat the pattern diagonally the opposite direction to create a "hatchmark" pattern in the chocolate. Use a French style knife to cut the squares apart. Refrigerate or freeze uncovered for a few minutes to harden the milk chocolate. Serve at room temperature or chilled.

A

B

CHOCOLATE SPARROWS

An elaborate version of Chocolate Squares, these were a rare treat that we sometimes made at Easter time, if the mood arose. The novelty of the bird shape can make for some fun conversation.

Makes 12 sparrows.

Prepare Viennese Wafer Dough (page 45) and refrigerate for a couple of hours or overnight.

Prepare Canache (page 44) and let cool to room temperature, then chill for an hour or overnight. Do not whip yet.

24 roasted almond slivers or 12 whole roasted almonds
23 ounces milk chocolate or milk chocolate coating
   (3-½ cups chips)
2-½ teaspoons vegetable oil

Preheat oven to 300°.

If not purchased already roasted, roast the almonds for 10-12 minutes. On a lightly floured surface, roll the Viennese Wafer dough out until it is ¼ inch thick. Use a 2 inch round cookie cutter (or whatever round container or glass will work) to cut 26 circles. Place all of them onto a parchment lined baking sheet. Leave 12 of them whole, cut 12 of them in half, then cut two of them into 6 pie-shaped pieces. **(A)** Bake for 20-35 minutes or until the edges begin to brown. Let cool to room temperature.

A   B

Whip the canache according to the recipe (allow yourself plenty of time in case temperature corrections are needed to get the proper consistency.) Use a spatula to fill the canache into a pastry bag or plastic sandwich bag with a ½ inch opening cut across one corner. Imagine that you are creating a very small, two-piece chocolate

snowman with neck problems. Pipe a large round blob of the canache onto one of the whole Viennese circles. Slightly off-center, pipe a smaller round blob. Stick two almond slivers or a whole almond into the front of the "head" to create a beak. Stick two of the half-circle pieces into the "body", the rounded portion facing towards the "head", to create wings. Stick the pointed end of a pie-shaped piece into the "body" between the wings to create a tail. **(B)** Repeat this process one bird at a time; resist the temptation to pipe the bodies, then add the parts, as the canache will harden too quickly. Freeze the birds until hard (approximately 20-30 minutes).

Melt the milk chocolate by using a double-boiler over low-medium heat or microwaving it, then stirring it, in 5-10 second intervals. Use a wire whip to stir the vegetable oil into the chocolate. Before dipping them, remove the birds from the freezer and let them sit at room temperature for 3-5 minutes. (If they are too cold, the chocolate coating will crack.) To dip the birds, put the warm chocolate into some kind of container that is deep and wide enough for the entire bird. It does not necessarily need to hold all of the chocolate at once, but can be refreshed after dipping a couple of birds. To dip the birds, take hold of the bottom circle and turn it upside down and dip it into the chocolate. Hold it over the chocolate long enough for any excess chocolate to drip off. Place the bird right side up onto a parchment lined sheet or onto a rack with a pan underneath to catch any chocolate drippings (which can later be scraped off and used again). It will be necessary to melt more chocolate than will actually be needed to cover the birds. Put any leftover chocolate into a container you won't miss too much, let it cool at room temperature, cover it with plastic and store it in a cool, dry place until you need melted chocolate once again.

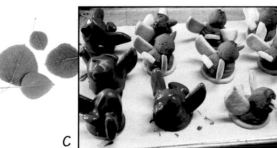

C

Délice

RAGUSA

This yummy hazelnut chocolate bar is Walter's interpretation of chocolates that he and Viola tasted on a trip to Switzerland to visit Walter's family.

The crust can be baked ahead, but if it has been refrigerated or frozen, it is imperative that it be allowed to reach room temperature before the chocolate is spread onto it. If the crust is cold, the chocolate will not stick. The hazelnut praliné (candied hazelnuts) can also be prepared ahead of time.

Makes 16 bars.

Prepare Viennese Wafer Dough (page 45) and refrigerate several hours or overnight. You will need half of it.

Prepare Canache (page 44) and let cool to room temperature, then chill for an hour or overnight. Do not whip yet.

2 cups hazelnuts (filberts)
4 tablespoons sugar
8 ounces milk chocolate or milk chocolate coating, divided (a generous 1 cup of chocolate chips)
¼ teaspoon vegetable oil

The crust:
Preheat oven to 300°.

Have a 9 x 9 inch baking pan handy. On a lightly floured surface, roll ½ of the Viennese Wafer dough out until it is ¼ inch thick. Lightly flour the surface of the dough. To lift it, roll it around your rolling pin or fold it twice. Carefully lift it and unroll or unfold it out over the baking pan. Use a dough cutter or a knife to cut the dough the size of the pan bottom.

Bake for 25-35 minutes, turning the pan around once, until the edges and spots across the middle begin to brown. Should the dough begin to "bubble", use a knife or toothpick inserted into the bubble to let the steam out. Let cool to room temperature. Leave in the pan.

Hazelnut praliné:
Preheat oven to 325º.

Spread all of the unroasted hazelnuts into a metal loaf pan or small baking pan and place in the oven for 6-10 minutes or just until they begin to brown. (If hazelnuts are already roasted, skip this step.) Let them cool and rub as much of the papery shells off as you can. Set 1 cup aside.

Have a metal baking or cake pan handy. Measure the sugar and place it, and the other cup of the roasted nuts, near the stove. Heat a heavy saucepan on low heat. Have a wooden spoon handy for stirring. Sprinkle just a little bit of the sugar into the bottom of the pan. Wait for the sugar to begin to melt. Resist the temptation to turn the heat up, no matter the seeming eternity of waiting. Once the sugar does begin to melt, sprinkle the remaining sugar into the pan a teaspoon or two at a time. Let each sprinkle melt before adding more. Stir as needed, to keep the already melted sugar from becoming too dark. Once all of the sugar has melted and no longer has a granular texture, stir ¾ cup of the nuts in. Stir until the nuts are well coated. Be careful not to get any of the caramelized sugar on your fingers, as it really burns. As best you can, spread the candied nuts out on the baking or cake pan. Pour the remaining ¼ cup of nuts into the residual caramelized sugar in the pan and coat them as well. Remove them to the baking or cake pan with the rest. Let cool 15-20 minutes. Break or cut the candied nuts into small pieces.

If available, use a grinder or food processor to grind the pieces of candied hazelnut into a rough meal. If not, use a knife to cut the pieces as small as possible. Set the resulting hazelnut praliné aside.

continued on next page...

Putting it all together:

Whip the canache according to the recipe, allowing time for several temperature corrections if necessary.

While the canache is whipping, melt half of the milk chocolate. If not using chocolate chips, cut or break the milk chocolate into pieces. Use a double-boiler over low-medium heat or microwave the chocolate in 5-10 second intervals, stirring the chocolate between each interval. In a large bowl, stir together the whipped canache, the melted milk chocolate, the hazelnut praliné and the remaining cup of whole roasted hazelnuts. Use a spatula to spread this mixture over the baked crust. Melt the remaining milk chocolate. Stir the vegetable oil into the chocolate and spread the chocolate thinly over the canache/hazelnut in the pan. Use the edge of the spatula to create a crosshatch pattern in the milk chocolate before it hardens. Refrigerate for 20-30 minutes. Cut into bars or squares using a French style knife.

Viola behind the pastry counter at the Glenwood Springs store

Délice

CHOCOLATE COATED CANDIED NUTS

If you really want to impress your family, friends or co-workers, take them homemade chocolate candies; the kind that you would usually pay big bucks for. You will simply be paying in time instead of money.

I have given amounts and roasting times for both almonds and hazelnuts (filberts), but you can use whichever nuts you prefer (cashews don't do well) Keep in mind that the roasting times will be slightly different. The choice of dipping chocolate is also a subjective decision; try dark or even white chocolate. Honestly, the possible combinations are nearly endless. If you wish to really simplify, purchase the nuts already roasted, but not salted.

Makes approximately 3 cups of chocolates.

1-¼ cup whole hazelnuts or almonds
¾ cup sugar
8 ounces milk chocolate coating or milk chocolate
½ teaspoon vegetable oil

Preheat oven to 325º.

Spread unroasted nuts into a metal loaf pan or small baking pan and place in the oven for 10-15 minutes. (Skip this step, if nuts were purchased roasted.) If using hazelnuts, let them cool and rub as much of the papery shells off as you can.

Have a baking pan or plate handy. Measure the sugar and place it, and the roasted nuts, near the stove. Heat a heavy saucepan on low heat. Have a wooden spoon handy for stirring. Sprinkle just a little bit of the sugar into the bottom of the pan. Wait for the sugar to begin to melt. Resist the temptation to turn the heat up, no matter the seeming eternity of waiting. Once the sugar does begin to melt, sprinkle the remaining sugar into the pan a teaspoon or two at a time. Let each sprinkle melt before adding more. Stir as needed to keep the already melted sugar from becoming too dark. Once all of the sugar has melted and it no longer has a granular texture, stir 1 cup of the nuts in until they are well coated. Be careful not to get any of the caramelized sugar on your fingers, as it really burns. As best you can, spread the candied nuts

out onto the baking sheet or plate. Pour the remaining ¼ cup of nuts into the residual caramelized sugar in the pan and coat them as well. Remove these coated nuts to the plate or baking sheet with the others. Let cool. Break or cut the candied nuts into small pieces.

Melt the chocolate by using a double-boiler over low-medium heat or microwaving it, then stirring it, in 5-10 second intervals. Stir the oil into the chocolate. It acts as a thinner and makes the final product more shiny. Line a sheet with parchment paper. Use a fork, tongs or your fingertips to dip the chunks of candied nuts into the chocolate. Scrape the excess chocolate off on the edge of the chocolate bowl. Place each dipped piece onto the parchment. Refrigerate or freeze to harden the chocolate.

Viola's chevy at Independence Pass Summit, 1959

1948 Swiss Army anti-aircraft gun training

Macaroons, Meringues and Miscellaneous Pastries

ALMOND MACAROONS

These are a very simple almond cookie that can be eaten plain or transformed into a true delicacy by sandwiching Lemon Creme between two of them and dipping one end into melted white chocolate. In springtime we would sometimes do a creative twist on these and make Green Chocolate Frogs.* For anyone who is wheat or dairy sensitive, these are a real treat.

Makes 15-20 cookies.

Prepare Lemon Creme (page 43), let reach room temperature and then chill an hour or overnight.

1 cup almond meal or flour (see Glossary)
¾ cup sugar
2 large egg whites
½ cup lemon creme
4 ounces white chocolate or white chocolate coating
   (or the chocolate of your choice)
½ teaspoon vegetable oil

Preheat oven to 250°.

Mix the almond flour with the sugar. Separate the egg whites from the yolks. Run a fork through the egg white several times to break up the egg white and make it easier to measure. Begin by adding 3 tablespoons of the egg white to the almond/sugar. Stir with a sturdy spoon. Add more egg white 1 teaspoon at a time, thoroughly mixing between each addition, only until the whole becomes a thick paste. Use a pastry bag or a plastic food bag with a corner snipped off to squeeze quarter or fifty-cent size portions onto a parchment lined baking sheet.

Bake for 30-40 minutes or until the cookies' edges brown. Leave on the tray to cool to room temperature. If they are difficult to remove from the parchment, freeze them briefly.

To layer the cookies, first turn half of them upside down. Use a pastry bag or a spoon to put a dollop of lemon creme on the flat side of each. Place one of the remaining cookies flat side toward the lemon creme on each one. Freeze them while you prepare the chocolate for dipping.

Melt the chocolate by using a double-boiler over low-medium heat or microwaving it, then stirring it, in 5-10 second intervals. Be careful not to overheat it, it only needs to be warm. Stir the vegetable oil into the chocolate to thin it. Line a tray or cookie sheet with wax paper or parchment. Scrape the chocolate into something that will make it deep enough to dip the cookies ½ to 1 inch deep. Dip one edge of each sandwich cookie in the chocolate, scrape any excess chocolate off on the edge of the chocolate container and place the cookie on the tray or sheet. If the chocolate runs low, use a pastry brush to brush it on. Chill briefly to harden the chocolate.

*GREEN CHOCOLATE FROGS

Find green chocolate or green chocolate coating.

Prepare Royal Frosting (page 46) and tint it pink.

Use a blob of royal frosting to glue two almond macaroons together at one edge so that they gape open like a clam. Cut a third almond macaroon in half and spread the two halves apart a bit, leaving them touching at one end. These will be feet. Use a blob of royal frosting to glue the "clam" onto the "feet" where they are touching. Use a pastry tube or plastic food bag with one corner cut off, to squeeze two round portions of royal frosting onto the top for eyes. Freeze until hard.

Melt the chocolate by using a double-boiler over low-medium heat or microwaving it, then stirring it, in 5-10 second intervals. Stir a few drops of vegetable oil into the chocolate to thin it. Dip the frogs into the chocolate and place them onto a parchment lined sheet or a grill placed over something to catch any chocolate drippings. (The drippings should be scraped up and stored for later use). Refrigerate until the chocolate hardens. Use a sharp paring knife to cut away the chocolate from the fronts of the eyes. Spread a thin layer of the pink royal frosting onto the "bottom" of the mouth. Serve and listen to the fun conversation.

Délice

COCONUT MACAROONS

These very simple cookies always seem to be a big hit. For an added flavor sensation, dip one end of each cookie into melted chocolate. This is the perfect dessert for those who are allergic to either wheat or dairy.

14 ounces sweetened coconut flake
²/₃ cup sugar
¼ cup (2 large) egg whites
2 tablespoons light corn syrup

Preheat oven to 350°.

Combine the ingredients and place into a double boiler, such as a metal or pyrex bowl sitting over a pan of water. Warm over medium heat, stirring occasionally for a half an hour. Remove from heat and let cool enough that it will not burn your fingers. Press the mixture into an ice cream scoop or spoon to create mounded cookies on a parchment covered or greased cookie sheet. Bake just until lightly browned, 10-12 minutes.

CORNETS

"Chocolate horns" are what most customers called these thin, crispy almond pastries filled with whipped chocolate (Canache) and dipped in chocolate. The process of baking and forming the Cornets can be frustrating; Walter inevitably voiced a number of Swiss expletives while creating them. The Cornet shape can only be rolled when they are hot, so working quickly with hot stuff can result in toasty fingertips. Be careful. Accept that not every Cornet will turn out perfectly.

Makes 16-20 cornets.

Prepare Canache (page 44) and let cool to room temperature, then chill for an hour or overnight. Do not whip yet. (An alternative to the whipped chocolate filling is the Lemon Creme, which should also be prepared and chilled for a couple of hours or overnight.)

½ tablespoon butter
½ cup + 1 tablespoon almond meal (see Glossary)
¼ cup sugar
3 tablespoons all-purpose flour
2 tablespoons water
1 tablespoon egg white
¼ teaspoon vanilla
1 – 1-½ cups whipped canache OR
1-½ - 2 cups lemon creme
3 ounces milk chocolate or milk chocolate coating
¾ teaspoon vegetable oil

Use a thin piece of plastic or cardboard to create a template for a 2-¾ - 3 inch diameter circle. Find a lid, soup can or glass that is the appropriate size. Draw around it to create the circle. Draw a circle around this one that is ½ inch larger. Drawing from two opposite sides of the larger circle, draw a raindrop-shaped "handle". Cut the entire raindrop shape out. Cut the inside circle away.

Preheat oven to 375°.

Melt the butter and use a pastry brush to generously spread it onto a metal baking sheet. Use a wire whip to mix together the almond meal, sugar, flour, water, egg white and vanilla.

Holding the template down on the buttered baking sheet, use a bent metal spatula to spread a thin layer of the almond mixture in the circle. Lift the template. Move the template over, place it back down onto the baking sheet and repeat the process until there are 6 or 8 almond circles on the sheet. **(A)**

continued on next page...

A

B

C

D

Place the sheet into the oven for 6-7 minutes. Have handy a thin pancake-turner type spatula, a large wooden spoon with a sturdy handle and a cutting board. Once a couple of the almond circles begin to brown around the edge and in spots across the middle, remove the baking sheet from the oven and sit it down. Quickly use the spatula to remove the darkest circle from the sheet and place it onto the cutting board. **(B)** Quickly wrap the circle around the end of the spoon handle so that it is shaped like a waffle ice cream cone. **(C)** Roll the circle so that the overlapping portions are facing down and use the spoon handle to press down and cause them to meld. **(D)** Set the rolled cornet aside and quickly scrape the darkest circle off of the baking sheet. Repeat

the rolling process. If you are lucky, you will be able to roll 2 or perhaps 3 cornets before the circles become too stiff to effectively roll. Place the baking sheet back into the oven just long enough to heat the remaining circles back up to temperature. Roll as many as you can, always choosing the darkest circle first. Reheat and roll any still on the sheet.

Once the first batch of cornets have been rolled, scrape the baking sheet and rebutter it generously. Use the template to create 6-8 more thin almond circles and bake them for 6-7 minutes. Roll and reheat them as needed. Repeat the entire process until all the almond mixture has been baked and rolled into cornets. Let cool for several minutes. Place the cornets onto a tray lined with parchment or wax paper.

If using canache, whip it according to the recipe, allowing time for several temperature corrections if necessary. Put the filling of your choice into a pastry bag or a large plastic sandwich bag with a half-inch cut made across one corner. (If using canache, using a large star tip will add appeal.) With a cornet in one hand, start squeezing the filling into the cornet as far back in as you can without danger of breaking the cornet. If using canache, swirl it as you move toward the opening of the cornet to give it a classier look. (Lemon creme will not hold a shape.) Place the cornet back onto the tray and repeat the filling process for all of them. Freeze until hard (approximately 20-30 minutes).

Melt the milk chocolate by using a double-boiler over low-medium heat or microwaving it, then stirring it, in 5-10 second intervals. Stir the vegetable oil into the chocolate. Dip the pointed one-third of each cornet into the chocolate at an angle. Scrape a bit of the excess chocolate off on the side of the bowl of chocolate and place each cornet back onto the tray. Refrigerate or freeze the dipped cornets momentarily to harden the chocolate.

Serve canache-filled cornets at room temperature (except perhaps in the heat of summer). Serve lemon creme-filled cornets chilled.

SABLES (PINWHEEL COOKIES)

Pronounced "Sob'lays", the word is French for sandy. These melt in your mouth cookies are swirls of chocolate and vanilla. Walter teasingly called them "Anaconda" because our recipe was so big that once they were rolled up, the roll was 3 inches thick and 4 or 5 feet long.

Makes 16-18 (2-¼ inch) cookies.

Prepare an eggwash (see Glossary) and refrigerate.

4 tablespoons butter
12 tablespoons margarine
2-²⁄₃ cups cake or pastry flour
²⁄₃ cup powdered sugar
1 teaspoon vanilla
2 tablespoons egg white (1 large egg)
2 tablespoons + 1 teaspoon cocoa powder

Cut the butter and the margarine into 5-6 chunks each. In a mixer bowl, assemble all of the ingredients except for the cocoa powder. Start mixing very slowly to keep the dry ingredients from flying. Mix just long enough for everything to come together. Remove approximately ¾ of the dough to a bowl. Add the cocoa powder to the remaining ¼ of the dough and mix just long enough to incorporate the cocoa powder. Scrape the chocolate dough into a separate bowl. Cover both bowls and refrigerate overnight or for several hours.

Preheat oven to 300°.

Line a baking sheet with parchment. On a lightly floured surface, roll the vanilla dough into a 9 x 11 inch rectangle. On another lightly floured surface roll the chocolate dough into a rectangle roughly the same size. **(A)** Brush the entire surface of the vanilla dough with eggwash. Lightly flour the surface of the chocolate dough and roll it around your rolling pin. Gently lift it and unroll the chocolate dough over the top of the vanilla dough. **(B)** Use your fingers to "make it fit" on the vanilla dough. Brush the entire surface of the chocolate dough with eggwash. Starting at one of the short edges, begin to roll the dough as you would a cake/jelly roll. **(C)** Be sure to make the first "curl" tight so that the cookies will not have a hole in the middle. Gently roll the final log a couple of times to even the dough out.

Use a French style knife to cut the roll into ½ inch slices. (If the dough "squishes" under the knife, refrigerate the roll for an hour, then slice it.) Place the swirls onto the baking sheet.

Bake for 40-45 minutes or until lightly brown around the edges.

A

B

C

LEMON BOATS

Why boats? Because originally these sweet treats were shaped like little boats. Over the decades the shape became simplified into what looked like the half of a very yellow egg. The "cookie" portion was created by bending a 2-½ inch round cookie cutter into the shape of an egg. Truly, the shape is not very important; it is the lemon creme's flavor that makes these pastries so memorable.

Fondant, the traditional "frosting" for Lemon Boats, can be purchased from the internet or specialty stores, but be sure to get the type used to coat petit fours, not rolled fondant. If this seems too complicated, a substitute glaze recipe has been included here, courtesy of Gale Gand (Food Network). If making 28 pastries at once seems a bit overkill, bake the cookies and make the lemon creme and the glaze. Freeze each separately and assemble as needed, or just freeze the finished boats for future cravings.

Makes 28 (2-½ inch long) lemon boats.

Prepare Lemon Creme (page 43) several hours ahead or the day before. Refrigerate.

Prepare Viennese Wafer Dough (page 45) several hours ahead or the day before. Refrigerate.

1-½ cups prepared Fondant OR:
⅓ cup corn syrup
⅔ cup hot water
3-½ cups powdered sugar
2-3 drops yellow food coloring
1 ounce milk chocolate coating or milk chocolate

The cookies:
Preheat oven to 300°.

Place oven rack high in oven. Line at least one baking sheet with parchment. Prepare a rolling surface by dusting it with flour. Roll half of the Viennese wafer dough out until it is less than ½ inch thick. Cut 30 cookies out of the dough. Place them onto one or more baking sheets. Reroll the remaining dough and cut more cookies from it, if necessary.

Bake for 25-30 minutes or until the edges begin to brown. Turning the baking sheet around in the oven once helps prevent uneven baking. Allow the cookies to cool to room temperature.

Assembly:
Using a large star tip in a pastry bag or in the corner of a plastic food bag, pipe the cold lemon creme onto the cookies. (A) Put the topped cookies into the freezer until the creme is hard.

Place a wire rack over a pan to catch drippings. Set it aside. Prepare 1-½ cups of fondant according to directions and stir in 2-3 drops of yellow food coloring. If not already warm, warm the fondant using a double boiler.

If using glaze instead, prepare it by first stirring the corn syrup into the hot water until dissolved. Mix this sweetened hot water into the powdered sugar. Color the glaze with 2-3 drops of yellow food color. There is no need to warm the glaze.

Carefully dip the frozen lemon boats, one at a time, into the warm fondant or room temperature glaze. Place the dipped pastries onto the wire rack. If the glaze is too thin, thicken it by adding ½ cup of powdered sugar. If the fondant is too thick and does not drip off onto the pan a little bit, stir in just a few drops of hot water. If the fondant or glaze becomes too shallow, tip the bowl to make the glaze or fondant "deeper", or place the undipped pastries onto the wire rack and spoon the fondant or glaze over them.

Melt the milk chocolate by using a double-boiler over low-medium heat or microwaving it, then stirring it, in 5-10 second intervals. Scrape the melted chocolate into a small plastic food bag . Cut a very tiny hole in one bottom corner of the bag and use it to drizzle a small zigzag pattern across the top of each pastry.

A

Refrigerate or freeze the lemon boats.

Délice

FRENCH NOUGAT

French Nougat is a sticky white relative of marshmallow that we mixed with whole roasted almonds and minced candied fruits. My nickname for it: nuts and fruits in Elmer's. When nougat was written on the "to do" board, we would save it for a day when not much else needed to get done because it monopolized the big mixer for a couple of hours. This home version is not so time consuming; it is Walter's ingredients, but the process is one modified from a similar recipe created by Emeril Lagasse.

You will need an electric mixer. The nougat can be prepared ahead, and once cool, can be wrapped in plastic and frozen for long periods of time before being cut and dipped in chocolate. Fruit cake mix is generally only available at the local grocery store during the holiday season, so buy a container of it to keep in your freezer.

Makes 24-33 bars.

1-½ cups (8 ounces) whole roasted almonds
1 cup chopped candied fruits (fruit cake mix)
1 teaspoon dark (gold) rum
2 egg whites, room temperature is best
1 cup sugar
⅓ cup honey
2 tablespoons light corn syrup
powdered sugar for dusting
12 ounces milk chocolate coating or milk chocolate
1-½ teaspoons vegetable oil

Roast the almonds, if needed (see Roasted Almonds, page 42). Measure the candied fruits into a bowl. Mix the rum into the candied fruit and set them aside. Line an 8 or 9 inch square pan with parchment, allowing the paper to extend up 2 opposite sides of the pan. (This will aid in removing the nougat from the pan later.) Place the egg whites into a mixer bowl, ready to whip. (Be sure that there is not the slightest amount of egg yolk in the whites since any fat in the egg whites will prevent them from whipping up.)

A brief warning about heated sugar: do not touch it no matter how tempting, because it will burn you. Have a small bowl of cold water handy. In a heavy saucepan, combine the sugar, the honey and the corn syrup. Heat over medium-low heat, while stirring occasionally, until the sugar is dissolved. Once the mixture boils, do not stir it. When the sugar comes to a full boil, start whipping the egg whites in the mixer. Continue to heat the sugar syrup for 4-5 minutes until it reaches the hard ball stage, which is when a small amount of the mixture dropped into the bowl of cold water forms a hard ball (250-260°). Remove the pan from heat and allow the foam to settle for a minute. The egg whites will have whipped up to a light foamy consistency. While the mixer continues to run, steadily drizzle approximately ½ of the sugar syrup into the whipping egg whites. Return the remaining syrup to the stovetop. Allow the egg white to mix. Continue to heat the remaining syrup until it reaches hard crack stage, which is when hard threads develop on blobs of the mixture dropped into the cold water (300°). Remove from heat and again let the foam settle for a moment. With the egg whites whipping, steadily drizzle the syrup into the egg whites. DO NOT try to scrape the syrup from the pan or scrape down the contents of the mixer bowl. Whip until the mixture begins to stiffen and will hold its shape when "stretched".

Using a sturdy spoon, fold the whole almonds and candied fruits into the mixture, being careful not to include the unmixed syrup that will have formed at the top edge. Avoiding the rim of unmixed syrup, scrape the mixture into the parchment-lined pan. **(A)** Place another sheet of parchment over the top of the mixture and press the nougat down into the pan. **(B)** Allow to cool completely at room temperature (1 hour). Freeze for 30 minutes.

A

B

continued on next page...

Line a metal or plastic sheet or tray with parchment. Sprinkle powdered sugar over the parchment. Sprinkle a cutting surface with powdered sugar. Peel the top sheet of parchment

C

from the nougat. Remove the nougat from the pan onto the cutting surface. Peel the parchment away from the square. Cut the square of nougat into 3 strips. Cleaning the knife, as needed, cut each strip into ½ inch slices. Place the slices onto the powdered sugar sprinkled, parchment-lined pan, "prettiest" side up. **(C)** Freeze the slices, uncovered, until hard (20-40 minutes).

Line another tray or sheet with parchment. Melt the milk chocolate by using a double-boiler over low-medium heat or microwaving it, then stirring it, in 5-10 second

intervals. Do not overheat it, just melt it. Mix the vegetable oil into the melted chocolate. Use a fork underneath a slice of the frozen nougat to dip it into the melted chocolate so that the top of the slice remains exposed. **(D)** Scrape excess chocolate off of the bottom of the slice by running the fork over the edge of the chocolate container. **(E)** Place the dipped slice onto the parchment-lined sheet. Repeat for all the slices.

Refrigerate or freeze briefly to harden the chocolate. Serve chilled. Store frozen in an airtight container or wrapped with plastic.

D   E

SHELLS

We called these sandwich cookies Shells because they were created to look much like a clam. We filled them with either Lemon Creme or Raspberry Jam, but you can fill them as you choose. The final touch is to dip one end of each sandwich cookie into melted chocolate to hold it all together.

The seashell appearance was created by piping the Soft Cookie Dough using a pastry bag with a star tip with a ½ inch opening. Although this is the ideal, realistically most of us don't have access to a decorating tip this size, so I have offered options for creating cookies that will not necessarily look like shells, but the flavor is still the same.

Makes 9-10 sandwich cookies, or 20 drop cookies.

Prepare the Soft Cookie Dough (page 45).

Prepare Lemon Creme (page 43) OR Raspberry Jam (page 125) or purchase a jam or jelly to use for filling.

⅓ – ½ cup jam, jelly or lemon creme
2-3 ounces milk chocolate
¾ teaspoon vegetable oil

Preheat oven to 325°.

Line a baking sheet with parchment. Use a pastry bag without a tip in it or a plastic sandwich bag with a corner snipped off, to pipe the dough onto the parchment lined baking sheet. Or, if you don't mind the rougher look, simply use a spoon to create drop cookies.

Bake for 28-32 minutes or until the edges and small areas across the middle of the cookies brown. Let cool to room temperature. Turn half of the cookies over and use a spoon or pastry bag to put a teaspoon-size dollop of the filling of choice on each overturned one. Use the remaining cookies to sandwich the filling. Freeze for 20-30 minutes.

Melt the chocolate by using a double-boiler over low-medium heat or microwaving it, then stirring it, in 5-10 second intervals. Use a wire whip to stir the vegetable oil into the chocolate. Dip one edge of each sandwich cookie into the chocolate and place it back onto parchment or wax paper. Refrigerate or freeze for a few minutes to harden the chocolate.

Délice

STICKS (ALMOND CINNAMON SHORTBREAD)

Sticks are a not-too-sweet refrigerator cookie that was the only recipe that we used baking powder for. A minimum of fuss. You can even keep the cookies in the freezer to bake at your convenience.

Makes 20 sticks.

½ cup + 2 tablespoons sugar
6 tablespoons butter
6 tablespoons margarine
1 cup sliced or diced roasted almonds (see Roasted Almonds, page 42)
½ teaspoon lemon zest (see Glossary)
2-½ teaspoons ground cinnamon
½ teaspoon vanilla
2 eggs
3-½ cups cake flour
3-½ teaspoons baking powder

Line a 9 x 9 inch baking pan with a sheet of parchment paper or wax paper so that the paper sticks up on two opposite edges. This will allow you to lift the dough out of the pan with ease later.

Cream together the sugar, the butter, the margarine, the roasted almonds, the lemon zest, the cinnamon and the vanilla. Scrape the bowl down at least once. Add the eggs and mix on medium speed. Add the flour and the baking powder. Mix only long enough to incorporate the dry ingredients. Press the dough into the paper-lined pan. Cover with plastic and refrigerate for 2 or more hours or overnight.

Preheat oven all the way to 325°.

Line a baking sheet with parchment. Remove the refrigerated dough to a cutting surface. Cut it once down the middle, then cut each resulting strip into ten slices, approximately ¾ inch thick. Place the slices onto the baking sheet, cut side up.

Bake for 25 minutes or until the cookies brown around the upper edges.

POPPYSEED POUNDCAKE

Our wedding cake was Poppyseed Poundcake layered with lemon butter creme (see Lemon Sponge Cake). Poundcake is delicious for breakfast or dessert, served with fresh strawberries or peaches and topped with whipped cream. We found out from one of our many employees that the poppyseeds can cause a positive response on some drug tests.

Makes 3 small loaves.

2 cups cake flour
4 tablespoons butter
12 tablespoons margarine
1 cup sugar
½ teaspoon lemon zest (see Glossary)
¼ teaspoon vanilla
3 tablespoons poppyseeds
1 cup eggs (5 large)

Preheat oven to 425°.

Grease three 3 x 6 inch loaf pans. Measure and sift the flour and set it aside. Melt just the butter. Cream together the melted butter, the margarine, the sugar, the lemon zest and the vanilla. Scrape the bowl down at least once. Add the poppyseeds and mix gently just until they are incorporated. Mixing slowly, add one egg and a bit of the flour. Mix gently until the egg and flour are incorporated. Repeat the process one egg at a time, mixing each egg in with a bit of the flour before adding the next. Gently mix in any remaining flour, only long enough to incorporate it. Divide the mixture between the three loaf pans.

Bake for 5 minutes at 425°, then turn the oven temperature down to 300° and bake for an additional 40 minutes. Let cool in the baking pans for 5-15 minutes before turning the loaves out.

CREAM PUFFS or CHOCOLATE ECLAIRS

Unlike custard-filled versions, our cream puffs and chocolate eclairs were filled with real whipped cream. We made them small, not so overwhelming. Once finished, they will actually survive for a couple of weeks in the freezer in an airtight container. It is important when preparing the filling that the egg whites be room temperature to maximize the whipped volume.

Makes 8 large or 15-20 small puffs or eclairs.

The puffs:

3 eggs
⅔ cup all-purpose flour
3 tablespoons sugar
¾ cup + 1 tablespoon water
3 tablespoons butter
2 ounces milk chocolate or milk chocolate coating
¼ teaspoon vegetable oil

Whipped cream filling:

1 pint (2 cups) heavy whipping cream
½ cup egg whites (4 large eggs) – room temperature
¼ teaspoon unflavored gelatin
¼ cup water
¾ cup + 2 tablespoons sugar
1-½ teaspoons light corn syrup
4 ounces bittersweet or semi-sweet chocolate
   (eclairs only)

The puffs:

Preheat oven all the way to 425º.

Line a baking sheet with parchment. Open the eggs into a small bowl and set them aside. Measure and sift the flour and set it aside. In a medium-sized saucepan, over medium heat, bring the sugar, water and butter to a full boil. Using a sturdy spoon (wooden is best), stir the flour in until it is completely absorbed and balls up. Remove from the heat and place the mixture into a mixer bowl. One at a time, mix the eggs in to the mixture in the mixer, whipping each one in before adding the next. Put the mixture into a pastry bag or a large plastic sandwich bag with a half-inch cut made across one corner. Onto the parchment-lined baking sheet, squeeze the mixture out into round portions for cream puffs or oblong portions

for eclairs. This recipe will make eight 3-inch puffs or twenty little ones, or whatever combination in between. Fifteen fit nicely onto an 11 x 17 inch baking sheet.

Once the puffs/eclairs are in the oven, DO NOT open the oven door, as this will allow all the steam to escape, and they will not puff. Bake for 15 minutes at 425º, then turn the oven down to 325º for an additional 18-20 minutes. Allow the puffs to cool to room temperature. Fill them right away or freeze them in an airtight bag or container until the right moment to fill them.

Use a knife with a serrated edge to cut the top off of each puff/eclair. Melt the milk chocolate by using a double-boiler over low-medium heat or microwaving it, then stirring it, in 5-10 second intervals. Stir the vegetable oil into the chocolate. Being sure to leave a bit of pastry showing around the edges, dip each top into the chocolate and place onto a tray. Put the dipped tops into the refrigerator momentarily to harden the chocolate.

The Whipped Cream filling:

Whip the whipping cream just until it thickens. Keep in mind that cream whipped beyond this stage becomes butter, so don't walk away from it. Place the whipped cream into a bowl and refrigerate it.

Separate the egg whites one at a time to be sure that not a drop of egg yolk is included. Place the egg whites, with the gelatin, into a very clean mixer bowl. Set them aside. In a medium-sized saucepan, mix the water, the sugar and the corn syrup. Begin whipping the egg whites on high speed. On medium-high heat, bring the sugar syrup to a full rolling boil. The moment the sugar syrup becomes "foamy" across the entire surface, remove it from the heat and immediately drizzle it slowly into the whipping egg whites. DO NOT scrape either the bowl or the pan. Let the mixture continue to whip until the outside of the mixer bowl is no longer warm to the touch (approximately 6-8 minutes). If making eclairs, melt the dark chocolate by using a double-boiler over low-medium heat or microwaving it, then stirring it, in 5-10 second intervals. Set it aside.

continued on next page...

CREAM PUFFS or CHOCOLATE ECLAIRS cont.

Using a rubber spatula, gently fold the refrigerated whipped cream into the egg white mixture. To create eclairs, place ¼ of the egg white/whipped cream mixture back into the whipped cream bowl and use a wire whip to gently mix the melted dark chocolate into it. Fold this chocolate cream back into the remaining egg white/whipped cream mixture.

Use a pastry bag or a large plastic sandwich bag with one corner snipped off, to pipe the whipped cream into the puffs/eclairs using a swirl pattern like an ice cream cone. Place the tops on. Serve right away, refrigerate briefly or freeze.

Walter's retirement party

Viola's maple leaf log cabin quilt done in the shades of the four seasons

CHOCOLATE or RASPBERRY MOUSSE

We offered individual servings of mousse in 3 ounce paper souffle cups. The cups were filled above the rim, then frozen. Before placing them in the refrigerated showcase, we quickly dipped the top in melted milk chocolate or put a couple of fresh or frozen raspberries on top. For a more classy presentation, put the mousse in decorative glasses, shave chocolate over the top and serve chilled or frozen with baked meringue cookies. Frozen mousse "cakes" were the mousse over a baked meringue base topped with chocolate shavings or drizzled with melted chocolate.

It is important that the egg white be room temperature to maximize the volume that it whips up to.

Makes approximately 4-½ cups or 1 mousse cake.

To create a mousse "cake", use Baked Meringue with Almond (page 83) to make one meringue cake base.

½ pint (1 cup) heavy whipping cream
¼ cup egg white (2 large eggs) – room temperature
½ teaspoon unflavored gelatin
2 tablespoons water
7 tablespoons sugar
¾ teaspoon light corn syrup
2 ounces dark chocolate (bittersweet or semi-sweet)
OR
¾ cup raspberry jam

Toppings:
chocolate bar for shavings
1-2 ounces chocolate for drizzling
fresh or frozen raspberries

Whip the heavy whipping cream until it forms peaks. Keep in mind that cream whipped beyond this stage becomes butter, so don't walk away from it. Place the whipped cream into a bowl, cover it with plastic and set it aside in the refrigerator.

Measure out the egg whites one at a time to be sure that no egg yolk is included. Place them, with the gelatin, into a very clean mixer bowl. Set aside. In a medium-sized saucepan, mix the water, the sugar and the corn syrup. Start whipping the egg whites on high speed. On medium-high heat, bring the sugar syrup to a full boil. The moment the sugar syrup looks "foamy" across the entire surface, remove it from the heat and immediately drizzle it into the whipping egg whites. DO NOT scrape either the bowl or the pan. Let the mixture continue to whip until the outside of the mixer bowl is no longer warm to the touch (approximately 6-8 minutes). (To make cleanup easier, soak the syrup pan with hot water.) To make chocolate mousse, melt the dark chocolate by using a double-boiler over low-medium heat or microwaving it, then stirring it, in 5-10 second intervals.

Using a rubber spatula, fold the refrigerated whipped cream into the egg white mixture. Place ¼ of the mixture back into the whipped cream bowl and use a wire whip to gently mix in the melted dark chocolate or the raspberrry jam. Add this flavored portion back into the remaining mixture and gently mix it all together.

Spoon the mousse into serving dishes or glasses. Refrigerate or freeze. Serve chilled or frozen, topped with chocolate curls or raspberries or both.

MOUSSE CAKE
Use Baked Meringue with Almonds (page 83) to make an 8 inch circle base .

Line an 8 or 9 inch cake pan with plastic wrap. Pour or spoon the mousse into the pan. Place a baked meringue circle, flat side up, onto the mousse and press lightly. Freeze until hard (approximately 2 hours).

To remove the mousse from the pan, dip the pan very briefly into a bowl of hot water and invert. Remove the plastic wrap. Drizzle with melted chocolate or shave chocolate curls on the top. Serve frozen. To slice the cake, warm a knife by running hot water over the blade, then wipe it dry before cutting.

Délice

BAKED MERINGUE WITH ALMOND

We used this type of Baked Meringue underneath all of the cakes, as the base for the infamous Sarah Bernhardts, and as the "bun" portion of the Hotdogs. It is a sturdier version of the Holiday Baked Meringue.

It is important that the egg whites be room temperature, as this allows for the maximum amount of volume increase when they are whipped. The slightest bit of fat in the mixing bowl or on the whip may affect the outcome, as will the smallest bit of egg yolk. So, mixing in a stainless steel or glass bowl is recommended. Avoid plastic. Separate each egg individually, so that if one egg white ends up with yolk in it, you can replace it.

Makes 2 (8-9 inch) cake circles or approximately 15-25 meringues.

¼ cup cake flour (all-purpose will work)
¼ cup almond flour or meal (see Glossary)
7 tablespoons sugar
¼ cup egg white (2 large eggs)

Preheat oven all the way to 250°.

Place oven rack near the top. Line a baking sheet with parchment. Do not start mixing the eggs until the oven has reached temperature and all your ingredients are assembled. Measure the flour and the almond flour, stir them together and set them aside. Measure the sugar and set it aside. In a mixer, whip the room temperature egg whites on high speed with one tablespoon of the sugar. It will get foamy first, then begin to thicken and turn white. Allow it to mix for 5-7 minutes. Add the remaining sugar and count slowly to ten. Stop the mixer. Using a rubber spatula or your hand, fold in the cake/almond flour mixture, being careful not to "squish" the air out of the whipped mixture.

Individual Meringues:

Use a pastry tube without a tip in it or a plastic sandwich bag with one corner snipped off, to pipe the meringues on the parchment lined baking sheet. For additional texture, dust them lightly with almond flour. Bake for 20 minutes at 250°. Turn the oven off and leave the meringues in for an additional 30 minutes. Let cool before handling.

Cake Bases:

Use whichever cake pan you intend to use for your cakes as a pattern to draw 2 circles on the parchment that will line the baking sheet. Divide the meringue between the 2 circles and spread it to just inside the drawn lines. **(A)** If you only need one cake base, simply pipe the remaining meringue into individual meringues on the same sheet. Bake for 30 minutes at 250°. Turn the oven off and leave the meringue in the oven for an additional 30 minutes. Let cool before handling.

A

HOTDOGS

Why call them hotdogs? Because they look just like little bitty hotdogs; two baked meringue "buns" filled with Canache. They are the proportional opposites of the Sarah Bernhardts: more Meringue, less Canache.

Just like the Sarah Bernhardts, you are likely to end up with either leftover whipped Canache or leftover Baked Meringues. The meringue recipe can be affected by such nebulous factors as the eggs' temperatures or the ambient humidity. The volume to which the Canache eventually whips up to is equally unpredictable. However, someone is generally happy to eat any leftovers.

Prepare Canache (page 44) and let cool to room temperature, then cover and refrigerate for an hour or overnight. Do not whip yet.

Prepare a double recipe of Baked Meringue with Almonds (page 83).

When piping the meringue mixture onto a parchment lined baking sheet, create portions that are approximately an inch wide and 2 or 2-½ inches long. Sprinkle them lightly with almond flour before baking. Bake as directed.

Let the meringues cool before handling. Do not refrigerate the meringues. If you make them ahead, simply roll them up in the parchment paper and put them into a plastic bag and leave them at room temperature. They will be good for several days.

Whip the canache according to the recipe, allowing time for several temperature corrections if necessary. Meanwhile, turn half of the meringues over so that the flat side is exposed. Put the whipped canache into a pastry bag or plastic sandwich bag with a half-inch cut made across one corner and pipe a chocolate "tube" the length of each meringue. Without delay, sandwich the chocolate with another meringue and press them gently together so that the chocolate nearly reaches the edges. To store, freeze in an airtight container. Serve at room temperature, as long as it is not very hot.

HOLIDAY BAKED MERINGUES

Baked meringues are so light that you can eat several of them and never feel full. Sold only during the holiday season, vanilla, coffee and chocolate flavors were included in each plastic bag. Our meringues were shaped much like the tops of soft-serve ice cream cones, but meringue can be whatever shape or size you pipe it into (see also Meringue Mushrooms or Baked Meringue with Almonds).

It is important that the egg whites be room temperature. They will whip up to a greater volume. Avoid plastic mixing bowls. Mix in a stainless steel or glass bowl, since the slightest bit of fat in the mixing bowl or on the whip may affect whether or not the eggs will whip up. Separate each egg individually, so that if one egg white ends up with any yolk in it, you can carefully remove the bit of egg yolk or replace that egg white altogether. The smallest bit of egg yolk may prevent the egg whites from whipping up.

¼ cup egg whites (2 large eggs)
½ cup sugar
½ teaspoon corn starch

one of the following flavorings:
¾ teaspoon vanilla
1 tablespoon cocoa powder
1 tablespoon coffee strengthened with 1 teaspoon Folger's Coffee Crystals

Preheat oven to 225°.

Place the oven rack near the top. Line a baking sheet with parchment. Do not start mixing the eggs until the oven has reached temperature and all your ingredients are assembled. Measure the sugar and set aside. Measure and set aside the corn starch and your choice of flavoring. If using cocoa powder, sift it. Separate the eggs. In a mixer, whip the egg whites on high speed for 5 to 7 minutes. Without turning the mixer off, add the sugar and let it whip while you count to 7 or 8. Use a rubber spatula to fold the corn starch and flavoring in by hand.

Use a pastry tube or a plastic sandwich bag with one corner snipped off, to pipe the meringue onto the parchment lined baking sheet. Bake for 1 hour. Turn the oven off and leave the meringue in the oven for an additional hour or even overnight. Let cool to room temperature before handling.

Keep in an airtight container at room temperature for several days.

Délice

MERINGUE MUSHROOMS

Each of our Christmas Gingerbread Houses had four mushrooms, two on each side. Fragile but fun, these are baked in two pieces and "glued" together using Royal Frosting. If you are indeed using these to decorate a Gingerbread House, wait to assemble them once you have whipped up the Royal Frosting to assemble the house with, instead of making the frosting just to put the mushrooms together.

It is critical that the egg whites be room temperature, as this allows for the maximum amount of volume increase when they are whipped. The slightest bit of fat in the mixing bowl or the whip may affect the outcome, as will the smallest bit of egg yolk. Thus, mixing in a stainless steel or glass bowl is recommended. Avoid plastic. Separate each egg individually, so that if one egg white ends up with yolk in it, you can replace it.

¼ cup egg whites (2 large eggs)
½ cup sugar
½ teaspoon corn starch
¾ teaspoon vanilla
Royal Frosting (for assembly)

Preheat oven to 225° and place oven rack near the top.

Line a baking sheet with parchment. Do not start mixing the eggs until the oven has reached temperature and all your ingredients are assembled. Measure the sugar and set aside. Have the corn starch and vanilla handy. In a mixer, whip the room temperature egg whites on high speed for 5 to 7 minutes. Without turning the mixer off, add the sugar and let it whip. Count slowly to 8 and turn the mixer off. Use a rubber spatula to gently fold the cornstarch and vanilla into the whipped egg white by hand.

A

Use a pastry tube or a plastic sandwich bag with one corner snipped off, to pipe the same number of tops and bottoms onto the parchment lined baking sheet. The bottoms should be shaped just like chocolate kisses and the tops, well, the shape of a mushroom top. **(A)** Sprinkle the tops lightly with cocoa powder or cinnamon. Bake for 1 hour. Turn the oven off and leave the meringues in for an additional hour or even overnight. Let cool before handling.

To assemble:
Prepare Royal Frosting (page 46).

Make a small indentation in the flat side of one top and pinch the peak off of one bottom. Put a dab of royal frosting either in the dent in the top or at the peak of the bottom. **(B)** Insert the tip of the bottom into the dent in the top. (Some breakage is inevitable.) Repeat the process for each mushroom. Let the frosting harden.

Do not freeze or refrigerate. Store in an airtight container at room temperature.

B

The front counter at the second Aspen store

Bars and Pies

1967 Aspen Times Magazine cover

VIENNESE WAFERS

Viennese Wafers are a layer of Raspberry Jam sandwiched between two layers of light almond crust and dressed with just a touch of chocolate. A lightly sweet dessert, they lack the intensity of many of the heavier pastries. Although our traditional shape was a square, if you don't mind filling each one individually, the dough can be rolled out and cut with the cookie cutter of your choice.

Makes 24-30 rectangles or squares.

Prepare Viennese Wafer Dough (page 45) and refrigerate for several hours or overnight.

½ cup raspberry jam (page 125)
1 ounce milk chocolate coating or milk chocolate

Preheat oven to 300°.

Place baking rack high up in the oven. Have handy an 11 x 17 inch rimmed baking sheet.

Prepare a rolling surface by dusting it with flour. Roll the Viennese wafer dough out into a large rectangle, approximately ¼ inch thick. Dust the top of the dough. Carefully roll the dough around your rolling pin and lift it. Unroll the dough very gently over the baking sheet. Use your fingers to press the dough together wherever it may have torn. Use a knife or dough cutter to cut the dough to fit the bottom of the baking sheet. Measure or "eyeball" the center of the dough and cut it in half. Leave one half whole. Use a French style knife or dough cutter to cut the other half into rectangles of whichever size you wish the final pastries to be.

Bake for 25-30 minutes or until the edges begin to brown. Turn the baking sheet around in the oven once. Should the dough begin to "bubble", carefully use a knife or toothpick inserted into the bubble to let the steam out. Let cool to room temperature.

Spread the raspberry jam completely over the 'whole', or uncut, half. Place the rectangles over the top of the raspberry jam. Melt the chocolate by using a double-boiler over low-medium heat or microwaving it, then stirring it, in 5-10 second intervals. Spoon the chocolate into a plastic sandwich bag. Cut a very tiny corner off of the bag and drizzle the chocolate back and forth across the entire large rectangle, first in one direction, then the opposite. Use a French style knife to cut the rectangles apart. Refrigerate or freeze uncovered for several minutes so that the chocolate hardens. Serve at room temperature.

Donna, the best listener in the building

Délice

CREAM CHEESE BARS

These baked cream cheese bars are like a few bites of cinnamon cheesecake. We always served them in small rectangular portions that were fairly thin. When testing this recipe, I inadvertently discovered that if you fix them in a smaller 9 x 9 inch baking pan they are much thicker and even more reminiscent of cheesecake.

Makes 16-20 bars.

1 cup cake flour
1-½ tablespoons butter
5 tablespoons margarine
¼ teaspoon lemon zest (optional)
½ teaspoon lemon juice
¼ cup sugar
⅛ teaspoon vanilla
3-¾ teaspoon milk
2 eggs
1 pound (16 ounces) cream cheese
1 cup sugar
2 tablespoons apricot jam or syrup
1-¼ cup powdered sugar
1-¼ teaspoon ground cinnamon
2 tablespoons hot water

The crust:
Preheat oven to 300°.

Measure and sift the flour and set aside. Melt just the butter. Cream together the melted butter, margarine, lemon zest, lemon juice, sugar and vanilla. Begin on low speed. Scrape the bowl down at least once. Once the ingredients are mixed, whip the mixture on a higher speed for a minute or two to make it lighter and fluffier. Add the milk. Open an egg into a small bowl, stir it with a fork, then measure 1-½ tablespoons of it into the mixture. (Discard or store the rest of the egg.) Again, start on low speed, scrape the bowl down at least once, then whip for a couple of minutes until it is light and fluffy. Add the flour and mix on low speed just long enough to incorporate the flour. Do not overmix. Spread the dough into the bottom of a 9 x 13 inch baking pan. Set it aside.

The cream cheese layer:
Cream together the cream cheese, sugar and one egg. Spread the mixture evenly over the crust in the pan.

Bake for 1 hour or until the top begins to lightly brown across the middle. If the cheese layer develops a large air bubble, carefully perforate the bubble with the tip of a knife or a toothpick.

While the bars are baking, measure the apricot jam into a microwave-safe bowl. Prepare a glaze by mixing the powdered sugar, cinnamon and hot water. Set it aside. Have a pastry brush and a spatula handy.

Remove the bars from the oven. Microwave the apricot jam or syrup to a boil. Use the pastry brush to gently brush the jam or syrup over the top of the baked cream cheese. Over this, pour and spread the cinnamon glaze (the heat will thin the glaze). Let cool to room temperature, then refrigerate before cutting into squares or rectangles.

LECKERLE

Leckerle is a cousin to gingerbread, but the inclusion of Candied Lemon Rind gives it a more subtle, sophisticated flavor. The Candied Lemon Rind may be time consuming to create from scratch, but a little bit goes a very long way. A commercial version of chopped Candied Lemon rind may be available during the holiday season at the local market or from the internet. Homemade or purchased, it can be kept frozen indefinitely. In a real pinch, substitute a teaspoon of lemon zest.

Makes 16-20 bars.

Prepare Candied Lemon Rind (page 46) or purchase a commercial version.

Roast almonds, if necessary (see Roasted Almonds, page 42).

²⁄₃ cup sliced roasted almonds
²⁄₃ cup honey
9 tablespoons sugar, divided
1 tablespoon candied lemon rind
3 cups cake flour
1 teaspoon baking soda
¼ teaspoon salt
1 tablespoon ground cinnamon
¼ teaspoon ground clove
pinch ground nutmeg
1 egg
1 tablespoon water
½ teaspoon light corn syrup (optional)

Preheat oven to 375°.

Line the bottom of a 9 x 13 inch baking pan with parchment. Dust the parchment heavily with flour and set the pan aside. Into a small saucepan, measure the honey and 5 tablespoons of the sugar. Set it aside. If mixing by hand, chop the roasted almonds with a knife or in a food processor and place into a large mixing bowl. If using a mixer, skip the chopping and add the almonds directly into the mixer bowl. Chop the candied lemon rind into very small bits and add it to the almonds. Also add the cake flour, baking soda, salt, cinnamon, clove, nutmeg,

and the egg . Mix just long enough to stir everything together. Heat the honey/sugar over medium heat just until it begins to boil. While stirring slowly, add the warm honey/sugar to the "dry" ingredients until well blended.

Scrape the sticky dough out onto a well-floured surface. Flour your hands and knead the dough a couple of times. Keeping everything floured to prevent sticking, roll the dough out into a rectangle that will fit into the baking pan. Move the dough to the baking pan. Use your fingertips to shape it to fit the pan.

Bake for 15 minutes or until browning begins to occur across the middle of the dough, not just on the edges. While the dough is baking, measure 4 tablespoons of sugar, 1 tablespoon of water and the corn syrup (if you have it) into a heavily-bottomed saucepan and set aside. Have a pastry brush handy.

Immediately upon removing the baked leckerle from the oven, heat the sugar/water (syrup) over medium heat. First bring it to a boil. Allow it to boil until it becomes foamy across the entire surface. Test the sugar every few seconds to determine if it has reached the correct temperature, by using the pastry brush to quickly apply a dab of the sugar syrup in a circular motion to the top of the pastry. The moment the syrup forms an opaque, white film on the pastry, remove the syrup from the heat and quickly apply it to the pastry, using a circular motion. Let cool to room temperature and cut into bars.

Délice

LINZER TORTE

Linzer Torte dough can be used in several different configurations, including the classic torte, chocolate glazed half-moons, or cookies. We served the half-moons frosted with cocoa-flavored fondant, which is difficult to find, thus a basic glaze recipe has been substituted. If you want the true flavor you can find fondant on the internet. You want the kind used to glaze petit fours, not the rolled fondant.

The dough:

3 tablespoons butter
6 tablespoons margarine
½ cup sugar
½ teaspoon vanilla
1 tablespoon ground cinnamon
½ teaspoon ground clove
1 teaspoon baking soda
1 ounce (¼ cup) sliced raw almonds
½ teaspoon lemon zest (see Glossary)
2-¼ cups cake or pastry flour
1 egg
2 tablespoons milk

Melt just the butter. Cream together the butter, the margarine, the sugar and the vanilla. Mix in the cinnamon, the clove, the baking soda, the almonds and the lemon zest. Be sure to scrape the bowl down at least once. Add the cake flour, the egg and the milk. Mix gently just long enough to create a thick dough. Place in a bowl and refrigerate for a couple of hours or overnight. The dough can also be frozen for long periods of time.

Linzer Torte:

Makes 1 (8 inch) torte.

Prepare an eggwash (see Glossary) and set aside.

½ cup raspberry jam
1 tablespoon sliced or slivered almonds

Preheat oven to 350°.

Have an 8 inch cake pan handy. On a lightly floured surface, roll the Linzer dough out until it is 3/8 – 1/2 inch thick. Lightly flour the surface of the dough and roll it around your rolling pin. Carefully roll it out over the cake pan. Lift the edge of the dough with one hand while carefully using the fingertips of the other hand to press the dough into the bottom edges of the pan. Cut the dough off approximately half way up the side of the pan. (A) Spread the raspberry jam on top of the dough in the pan. Set the pan aside. (B)

Roll the remaining dough out until it is ½ inch thick. Use a jagger (see Glossary) or a pizza cutter to cut ½ inch thick strips of the dough. (C) Use the strips to create a simple lattice pattern over the raspberry jam in the pan, leaving plenty of room between the strips for them to expand during baking. (D) Fold the outside edge of the dough down over the ends of the lattice strips. Use a pastry brush to brush the high points of the dough with eggwash. (E) Sprinkle the almonds randomly over the top. (F) (Use any remaining dough to make Linzer cookies.)

Bake the torte for 30-35 minutes or until the high points of the dough are well browned. Let cool before serving.

continued on next page...

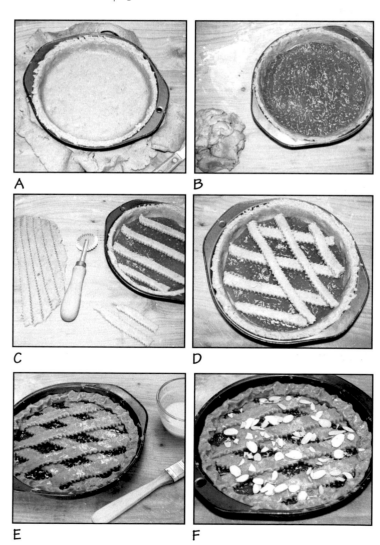

A

B

C

D

E

F

Half Moons:

Makes 12 half moons or bars.

¾ cup raspberry jam
1-½ tablespoons apricot jam or syrup (peach will work
  as well)
1 tablespoon cocoa powder
¼ cup prepared fondant OR:
¾ cup powdered sugar
4 teaspoons hot water

Preheat oven to 325°.

Cut a piece of parchment to fit the bottom of a 9 x 9 inch baking pan, to insure that the baked product will release from the pan. (If you don't have parchment, skip this step. It usually works without it.) Set the pan aside. On a lightly floured surface, roll the dough out in a square roughly ¼ inch thick. Flour the surface of the dough and carefully roll it around your rolling pin. Carefully roll it out over the baking pan. Lift the edge of the dough with one hand while carefully using the fingertips of the other hand to press the dough into the bottom edges of the pan, pressing the dough together to seal off any

tears. **(A)** Cut the dough off approximately half way up the side of the pan. Spread the raspberry jam on top of the dough in the pan. **(B)** Set the pan aside. Roll the remaining dough out until it is a square that will fit over the raspberry jam inside the pan. Fold the dough or use the rolling pin technique to move it into the pan. Gently tug it about to make it cover the jam completely. Trim the dough off that extends up the edges of the pan so that it is level. **(C)** (Use any remaining Linzer dough to make cookies.)

Bake the layered Linzer in the pan for 45-50 minutes or until it is well browned throughout. While it is baking, prepare the fondant (if needed) and flavor it with a tablespoon of cocoa powder. If not using fondant, prepare the glaze by sifting the powdered sugar and a tablespoon of cocoa powder together into a bowl. Use a wire whip to stir the hot water into the cocoa/powdered sugar. Sit the bowl over a small pan of simmering water (double boiler) for 5-10 minutes. Set the glaze aside. Put the apricot jam or syrup into a microwave-safe container and set it aside.

continued on next page...

A

B

C

D

LINZER TORTE cont.

Once the baked product is out of the oven, carefully invert it by placing a non-wooden cutting board, a tray, or a small baking sheet over the top and flipping the whole thing over. Lift the baking pan away. Microwave the apricot jam or syrup for 25-30 seconds. Use a pastry brush to brush the apricot over what is now the top of the square. Pour the chocolate fondant or glaze over the apricot. The heat from the pastry will cause it to thin. Spread the fondant or glaze over the top of the square. Set the whole aside until it cools to room temperature.

The half-moon shape was created by using a 2-½ inch scalloped biscuit cutter, but I always struggled with the seemingly unnecessary amount of "waste" that was created. I simply cut them into squares or rectangles, thereby allowing every delicious bite to be enjoyed. But, if you are a traditionalist, begin by using the cutter to take a ½ inch "bite" out of one edge. **(D)** Center the cutter over the bite in such a way as a half-moon shape is the result. Create half-moons across the square. Start with a "bite" each time you begin at the edge. Dip the cutter in a bowl of warm water in between cuts to make cleaner edges.

Linzer Cookies:
Makes 20 (2-½ - 3 inch) cookies.

Prepare an eggwash (see Glossary) and set aside.

⅓ cup almond slivers, roasted or raw

If baking right away, preheat oven to 325°.

Roll the dough out on a lightly floured surface until ¼ inch thick. Use a large, round, scalloped cookie cutter to cut as many cookies as possible, leaving them on the rolling surface. Pull away the extra dough and set it aside. Brush each cookie with eggwash. Sprinkle each with slivered almonds. **(A)** Gently use a rolling pin to roll the almonds into the cookies. Place these cookies onto a baking sheet giving them enough room to expand, or freeze them to bake at a later date. Roll out the remaining dough and repeat the process until all the dough has been used.

Bake for 20-25 minutes or until browned around the edges.

A

Délice _____

PECAN PIE OR WALNUT BARS

Pecan Pie was served by the slice or whole ones were available from the freezer showcase. The only difference between the pies and the bars is the choice of nuts sprinkled liberally across the top before baking. Walter's major complaint about the bars was that, because the oven was not perfectly flat, one corner of the walnut bar sheet would often be devoid of nuts since they flowed to the lower corner during baking.

Makes 1 (8 inch) pecan pie or approximately 24-27 walnut bars.

Prepare Viennese Wafer Dough (page 45) the day before or several hours ahead. Refrigerate.

5 eggs
2-²/₃ tablespoons butter
2-²/₃ tablespoons margarine
½ pound (1-¼ cups lightly packed) light brown sugar
²/₃ cup light corn syrup
½ cup chopped pecans or walnuts for a pie, 1 cup
   for bars

Preheat oven to 350°.

Pie:

Have an 8 inch cake pan handy. On a lightly floured surface, roll half of the Viennese Wafer dough out until it is ¼ inch thick. Lightly flour the surface of the dough and either roll it around your rolling pin or fold it in half twice. Carefully lift the dough and unroll or unfold it out over the cake pan. Lift the edge of the dough with one hand while carefully using the fingertips of the other hand to press the dough into the bottom edges of the pan. Be sure to press the dough together anywhere the filling might leak out. Trim the dough off at the top edge of the pan. Set the lined pan aside in the refrigerator or other cool place.

Bars:

Have a 9 x 13 x 2 inch baking pan handy. To line the pan with the dough, lightly flour a rolling surface and roll ½ of the Viennese Wafer dough out into a rectangle that is ¼ inch thick. Lightly flour the surface of the dough. Roll it around your rolling pin. Lift it and carefully unroll it out over the baking pan. Lift the edge of the dough with one hand while carefully using the fingertips of the other hand to press the dough into the bottom edges of the pan. Be sure to press the dough together anywhere the filling might leak out. Use a dough cutter or knife to cut the dough off roughly ¾ inch down from the rim. Set the lined pan aside in the refrigerator or other cool place.

The filling:

Open the eggs into a bowl and use a wire whip to beat them. Set them aside. In a large cooking pot with a flat bottom, melt the butter and the margarine over medium heat. Use the wire whip to stir the brown sugar and the corn syrup into the melted butter/margarine. Stirring occasionally, bring the mixture to a full boil. All at once, add the beaten eggs to the boiling ingredients and stir vigorously with the whip. Stir constantly to keep the mixture from attaching to the bottom of the pan, until it returns to a full boil. Remove it from the heat. Let it cool at least 10 minutes.

Ladle or pour the filling into the dough-lined cake or baking pan. Sprinkle the pecans or walnuts evenly over the surface of the filling.

Bake for 35-50 minutes or until the center no longer jiggles and the edges begin to brown. Let cool to room temperature. It can be helpful to refrigerate the bars before cutting them.

Délice

GRANDMA KINNE'S RHUBARB CUSTARD PIE

Walter modified this recipe from one handed down through Viola's side of the family. We never had to pay for rhubarb. Several of our customers would bring us their surplus, occasionally in 30 gallon bags. We would wash it, chop it into bite-size pieces and freeze it in small plastic bags. We sold the pies, by the slice or whole, as long as the summer's supply of rhubarb lasted.

If you need to organize ahead, line the cake or pie pans with dough and freeze them. Assemble the pie and bake when needed. Even easier, put everything together and freeze without baking. Let the frozen pie defrost in the refrigerator overnight and then bake it. If you are using frozen rhubarb, do not let it defrost but put it into the pies still frozen.

Makes two 8-inch pies.

Prepare Viennese Wafer Dough (page 45) and refrigerate for several hours or overnight.

3 cups fresh or frozen rhubarb
3 eggs
1-½ cups sugar
1-½ tablespoons all-purpose flour
1-½ tablespoons milk

Preheat oven to 325°.

If not already in small pieces, chop the rhubarb into bite-size pieces and set aside. Have handy two 8-inch cake or pie pans. Flour a rolling surface and gently roll half of the Viennese wafer dough until it is 3/8th inch thick. This is a very delicate dough. Should it tear, simply press it back together and lightly flour that spot. Lightly flour the top surface of the dough and roll it around your rolling pin to lift it over and unroll it over one of the cake pans. Very gently press the dough into the pan. Use a knife to cut the dough off at the top edge of the pan. Press bits of dough over any tears or holes in the shell of dough in the pan to prevent the filling from oozing out. Add the dough that was cut away from the first pan to the remaining Viennese wafer dough and repeat the process to line the second cake or pie pan.

Spread the rhubarb evenly into the two dough-lined pans. In a bowl, beat together the eggs, the sugar, the flour, and the milk. Pour this mixture over the rhubarb in the pans.

Place the pies onto a rimmed baking sheet to catch any drips. Bake for 1 hour plus 10-20 minutes or until the middle of the pies no longer jiggles and the tips of some of the rhubarb are brown.

If you intend to remove a pie from the cake or pie pan to serve it, let it cool to room temperature. Run a knife or metal spatula between the crust and the rim of the pan. Place a cutting board or other flat object over the pie and carefully invert it. Remove the pan. Place a plate over the bottom and carefully flip it back over.

Before serving, sprinkle with cinnamon and sugar.

Visit to Grandma Kinne's, 1963

LEMONY RASPBERRY CHEESECAKE

This recipe is one that Walter modified from a Kraft recipe page in a TV Guide. We sold the cheesecake, by the slice or whole, with a lemony version of our homemade Raspberry Jam as topping. Making Raspberry Jam at home only takes minutes, but a store bought version of any jam will suffice, or top the cheesecake with fresh strawberries, raspberries or blueberries.

We prepared the crusts using our Soft Cookie Dough recipe, but if you really wish to simplify, a tasty alternative is to purchase 8-inch graham cracker crusts. If preparing the crusts yourself, they can be done the day before, wrapped in plastic and kept at room temperature or frozen.

Makes two 8-inch cheesecakes.

Prepare Raspberry Jam (page 125) or purchase the jam or fresh fruit of your choice.

Prepare Soft Cookie Dough (page 45) or purchase two graham cracker crusts.

16 ounces regular cream cheese
1 (3-ounce) package lemon Jello®
¾ cup boiling water
¼ cup cold water
½ pint (1 cup) heavy whipping cream
½ cup sugar
1 teaspoon vanilla

Homemade crusts:
Preheat oven to 325º.

On a piece of parchment, use the bottom of an 8-inch cake pan as a pattern to draw two circles. Place the parchment onto a large baking sheet. Dab a bit of the prepared soft cookie dough under each corner to "glue" the parchment to the sheet. Divide the soft cookie dough between the two circles and spread evenly within each marked circle. Bake for 30 minutes or until the edges and several places toward the middle become lightly browned. Let cool to room temperature.

The cream cheese filling:
Let the cream cheese reach room temperature, if possible. Have two 8-inch cake pans handy (or the alternative purchased crusts). In a small bowl, dissolve the package of lemon Jello® in the boiling water. Once the Jello® is completely dissolved, stir in the cold water and chill for 15-20 minutes. In a mixing bowl, whip the whipping cream just until it thickens (overwhipping will result in butter). Scrape it into another bowl and refrigerate it. Without necessarily cleaning the mixing bowl, use it for creaming together the cream cheese, the sugar and the vanilla until smooth and fluffy. Add the chilled lemon Jello® to the cream cheese mixture and mix on low speed until smooth, scraping the bowl at least once. Use a rubber spatula to gently fold the refrigerated whipped cream into the cream cheese/Jello® mixture.

Using homemade crusts:
Divide the filling between the 2 cake pans. Flat side up, place each crust onto the filling. Press very gently until the filling begins to squeeze up around the crust. If the crust cracks, it will not show in the end so do not be concerned. Freeze until hard.

To remove a frozen cheesecake from the cake pan, dip the cake pan into a bowl of hot water just for a moment then invert it onto a serving plate. Press on one edge of the cake pan bottom to bend the pan slightly.

Add the topping of your choice and refrigerate for several hours or let sit at room temperature just long enough to defrost. Serve chilled.

Using purchased crusts:
Divide the cream cheese filling between the two crusts and even it out using a spatula. Refrigerate or freeze.

Add the topping of your choice while still cold. Serve chilled.

Délice

Cakes

The Gerbaz family's afternoon lunch break

STEPS TO ASSEMBLE A CAKE

A

B

C

D

E

F

G

Délice

CHOCOLATE FOR TOPPING CAKES

This is a topic that could potentially take up pages, but I will just offer up a couple of choices. Working with chocolate can be very scientific, but at the same time, very creative. Although we consistently used a particular chocolate for each type of cake, I encourage you to use the chocolate of your choice.

If you are the least bit curious, there are several books available about chocolate, its history, the process used to make it and using it in all its wonderful forms. It can be very helpful to find a book that describes the basic processes used to work with chocolate.

Drizzling Chocolate for two cakes:

Melt 4 tablespoons of chocolate chips in the microwave using 10 second and then 5 second intervals, stirring it between each period. Just melt it, do not let it get too hot. Stir in several drops of vegetable oil. Scrape into a small plastic snack or sandwich bag. Snip a very small opening across one of the bottom corners. Twist the top of the bag and drizzle the small stream of chocolate over the cake in the pattern of your choice. Or use it to write lettering. If you make a spelling error, let the chocolate cool and lift it off the cake with the tip of a knife or the tine of a fork and rework it.

Chocolate Shavings:

Scrape the edge of a chocolate bar with a vegetable peeler or paring knife to create curls. **(A)**

A

BLACK FOREST CAKE

There are no cherries in Walter's version of this classic European cake. Definitely the favorite of our cakes, during holidays we couldn't keep enough of these cakes in the display freezer.

There are a number of steps involved in getting a complete cake. I have found it helpful to bake the meringue bases ahead. You can even bake the sponge cakes ahead and freeze them until it is time to assemble everything. We kept the finished cakes frozen in the cake pans, ready to be topped or decorated with just a few minutes of work. I have been true to the process we used, but should you need the cake soon after assembly, reverse the assembly process without the cake pan. Begin with the meringue on the bottom, spread the chocolate cream over it and then layer and frost the cake as you would any other.

It is very helpful to have the eggs and egg whites at room temperature, in order to maximize the volume increase when whipping them. Without leavening, it is the air that lifts the sponge cake.

 Makes two 8-inch cakes.

Use Baked Meringue with Almond recipe (page 83) to create two 8-inch circle bases.

Chocolate Sponge Cake:
½ teaspoon butter
1 cup cake or pastry flour
3 tablespoons cocoa powder
½ cup sugar
2 tablespoons vegetable oil
1 cup eggs (5 large eggs) – room temperature

Whipped Cream Frosting:
½ pint (1 cup) heavy whipping cream
¼ cup egg white (2 large eggs) – room temperature
½ teaspoon unflavored gelatin
2 tablespoons water
7 tablespoons sugar
¾ teaspoon light corn syrup
1 ounce dark chocolate (semi-sweet or bittersweet)

bar of dark chocolate for decorative shavings

The sponge cake:

Preheat oven all the way to 350°.

Melt the ½ teaspoon of butter and use it to grease two 8-inch round cake pans. Measure and sift together the flour and the cocoa powder. Set them aside. Measure and set aside the sugar and then the oil. Begin whipping the eggs at medium speed. Add the sugar to the eggs. Once the sugar is in, turn the mixer up to high speed and let it go for 5-7 minutes. Use a rubber spatula to gently fold the flour in by hand. Next, add the oil. Fold it in by lifting it from the bottom of the bowl, folding it over, turning the bowl a bit and repeating the process. Be careful not to knock the air out of the mixture.

Divide the batter between the two greased cake pans. Bake for 15-20 minutes or just until the cake begins to brown and the edges begin to pull away from the pan. A gentle press of the fingers on the top should spring back. Let cool to room temperature before finishing or freezing.

Prepare the frosting and prepare to assemble:

Whip the heavy whipping cream until it forms peaks. Keep in mind that cream whipped beyond this stage becomes butter, so don't walk away from it. Place the whipped cream into a bowl and refrigerate it.

Measure out the egg whites one at a time to be sure that no egg yolk is included. Place them, with the gelatin, into a very clean mixer bowl. Set the bowl aside, ready to mix. In a medium-sized saucepan, mix the water, the sugar and the corn syrup. Start whipping the egg whites on high speed. On medium-high heat, bring the sugar syrup to a full boil. The moment the sugar syrup looks "foamy" all the way across the pan remove it from the heat and immediately drizzle it into the whipping egg whites. DO NOT scrape either the bowl or the pan. Let the mixture continue to whip until the outside of the mixer bowl is no longer warm to the touch. (To make cleanup easier, soak the pan with hot water.)

Délice

Using a rubber spatula, gently fold the refrigerated whipped cream into the egg white mixture. Melt the 1 ounce of dark chocolate by using a double-boiler over low-medium heat or microwaving it, then stirring it, in 5-10 second intervals. Scrape the melted dark chocolate into a large bowl. To the chocolate, add ½ cup of the whipped cream mixture and stir together with a wire whip. Once that is well mixed, stir in another ½ cup of the whipped cream. Set this chocolate cream aside.

Remove the sponge cakes from the pans and rub any loose cake from around the edges. Clean and dry the cake pans. Use a serrated knife to carefully cut the cakes horizontally across the middle.

To assemble (see photo sequence, page 98):
Place a large dollop of the white whipped cream mixture into each of the cake pans. Use a spatula to spread it over the bottom and all the way up the sides, being sure not to leave any "holes". **(A)** Place the top of one of the sponge cakes, cut side up, into the slathered pan. **(B)** Do the same for the second cake. Divide the remaining whipped cream mixture between the two cake pans, **(C)**

completely covering the cake, and spreading it all the way out to the edge of the pans. **(D)** Invert the remaining cake halves on top of the spread whipped cream mixture. **(E)**

Divide the chocolate whipped cream between the two cakes and spread thinly all the way out to the edges of the pans. **(F)** Place a baked meringue circle, flat side up, onto each and press lightly. **(G)** Cover each with a piece of plastic wrap. Freeze until hard. They will safely freeze for long periods of time.

To serve:
To remove a cake from the pan, dip the pan very briefly into a bowl of hot water and invert it. Press on one edge of the pan to push the cake out. As a last resort, use a knife to pry the cake out of the form, then use the same knife to patch any damage. Shave chocolate curls on the top (See Chocolate for Topping Cakes, page 99). For a birthday or special occasion, decorate with purchased decorating flowers. Serve chilled or semi-frozen. To slice the cake, warm a knife by running hot water over the blade, then wipe it dry before cutting.

LEMON SPONGE CAKE

Light yellow sponge cake layered with lemon butter creme, but Walter has finally allowed the secret ingredients to be revealed. They are rum and lemonade.

There are a number of steps involved in getting a complete cake. I have found it helpful to prepare and refrigerate the lemon creme the day before, as well as preparing and baking the meringue bases ahead. You can even bake the sponge cakes ahead and freeze them until it is time to assemble everything. I have been true to the assembly process that we used, but should you need the cake soon after assembly, do not use the cake pans. Begin with the meringue on the bottom and layer as you would any other cake.

It is very helpful to have the eggs at room temperature, in order to maximize the volume increase when whipping them. Without leavening, it is the air that lifts the sponge cake.

Makes two 8-inch cakes.

Use Baked Meringue with Almond (page 83) to create two 8-inch circles.

Prepare Lemon Creme (page 43) and refrigerate for at least an hour.

Yellow Sponge Cake:
½ teaspoon butter
1 cup + 2 tablespoons cake or pastry flour
½ cup sugar
2 tablespoons vegetable oil
1 cup eggs (5 large eggs) – room temperature

Lemon Butter Creme:
2 cups lemon creme
11 tablespoons unsalted butter
½ cup lemonade
1 teaspoon sugar
1 tablespoon dark (gold) rum

Milk Chocolate to shave or drizzle on top (see Chocolate for Topping Cakes, page 99).

The sponge cake:
Preheat oven all the way to 350°.

Melt the ½ teaspoon of butter and use it to grease two 8-inch round cake pans. Measure, sift and set aside the flour. Measure and set aside the sugar and then the oil. Begin whipping the room temperature eggs at medium speed. Add the sugar. Once the sugar is in, turn the mixer up to high speed and let it run for 5-7 minutes. Use a rubber spatula to gently fold the flour in by hand. Next, add the oil. Fold it in by lifting it from the bottom of the bowl, folding it over, turning the bowl a bit and repeating the process. Be careful not to knock the air out of the mixture.

Divide the batter between the two cake pans. Bake for 15-18 minutes or just until the cake begins to brown and the edges begin to pull away from the pan. A gentle press of the fingers on the top should spring back. Let cool to room temperature before finishing or freezing.

Prepare the frosting and prepare to assemble:
Prepare lemon butter creme by melting half of the unsalted butter. Place both the melted and unmelted butter into a mixing bowl. Whip it on low to medium speed until it is smooth. Add the lemon creme to the butter and mix until well incorporated. Scrape the bowl once in while. Set the frosting aside. In a small bowl, mix the lemonade, sugar, and rum. Set the mixture aside. Have a pastry brush handy. Remove the sponge cakes from the pans and rub any loose cake from around the edges. Clean and dry the cake pans. Use a serrated knife to carefully cut the cakes horizontally across the middle.

To assemble (see photo sequence, page 98):
Place a large dollop of the lemon butter creme into each of the two cake pans. Use a spatula to spread it over the bottom and all the way up the sides, being sure not to leave any "holes". **(A)** Place the top of one of the sponge cakes, cut side up, into the slathered pan. **(B)** Use the pastry brush to dab ¼ of the lemonade mixture over the cake half. Repeat the process for the second cake. Spoon additional lemon butter creme onto the soaked cake halves **(C)** (leaving approximately 1 cup of frosting

Délice

behind) and spread it evenly. **(D)** Invert the remaining cake halves onto the layer of lemon butter creme just spread into the cake pans and dab the remaining lemonade mixture onto them. **(E)** Divide the remaining lemon butter creme between the two cakes and spread over the bottom of each. **(F)** Place a baked meringue circle onto each and press lightly. **(G)** Cover each with a piece of plastic wrap. Freeze until hard. They safely freeze for long periods.

To serve:

To remove a cake from the pan, dip the pan very briefly into a bowl of hot water and invert it. Press on one edge of the pan to push the cake out. As a last resort, use a knife to pry the cake out of the form, then use the same knife to patch any damage. Shave chocolate curls on the top or drizzle with melted chocolate (See Chocolate for Topping Cakes). Decorate with purchased decorating flowers for a birthday or special occasion. Serve chilled. To slice the cake, warm a knife by running hot water over the blade, then wipe it dry before cutting.

Viola's crossstitch quilt in shades of pink and green

Louise and Walter in the back kitchen of the second store, 1960's

MOCCA SPONGE CAKE

Coffee butter creme is layered with light yellow sponge cake and finished with roasted almonds and drizzled or shaved milk chocolate. Walter created the coffee flavor using our regular brewed coffee boosted with Folger's coffee crystals. If the crystals are not in your pantry, simply brew a really strong cup of coffee or alternatively, just use the crystals in hot water to make the coffee.

There are a number of steps involved in getting a complete cake. I have found it helpful to bake the meringue bases a day ahead. You can even bake the sponge cakes ahead and freeze them until it is time to assemble everything. We kept the finished cakes frozen in the cake pans, ready to be topped or decorated with just a few minutes of work. I have been true to the process that we used, but should you need the cake soon after assembly, reverse the assembly process without the cake pan. Begin with the meringue on the bottom and layer as you would any other cake.

It is very helpful to have the eggs and egg whites at room temperature, in order to maximize the volume increase when whipping them. Without leavening, it is the air that lifts the sponge cake.

Makes two 8-inch cakes.

Use Baked Meringue with Almond recipe (page 83) to create two 8-inch circles.

Sponge Cake:
½ teaspoon butter
1 cup + 2 tablespoons cake or pastry flour
½ cup sugar
2 tablespoons vegetable oil
1 cup eggs (5 large eggs) – room temperature

Coffee Butter Creme:
½ cup egg whites (4 large eggs) – room temperature
¼ cup water
¾ cup + 2 tablespoons sugar, divided
1-½ teaspoons light corn syrup
13 tablespoons unsalted butter –
　room temperature is best

½ cup + 2 tablespoons strong brewed coffee
1 tablespoon + 1 teaspoon Folger's Coffee Crystals©
2 tablespoons dark (gold) rum

⅔ cups sliced, roasted almonds
　(see Roasted Almonds, page 42)
milk chocolate to shave or drizzle on top
　(see Chocolate for Topping Cakes, page 99)

The sponge cake:
Preheat oven all the way to 350°.

Melt the ½ teaspoon of butter and use it to grease two 8-inch round cake pans. Measure, sift and set aside the flour. Measure and set aside the sugar and then the oil. Open the eggs into a mixer bowl and begin whipping them at medium speed. Add the sugar. Once the sugar is in, turn the mixer up to high speed and let it run for 5-7 minutes. Use a rubber spatula to gently fold the flour in by hand. Next, add the oil. Fold it in with the rubber spatula by lifting it from the bottom of the bowl, folding it over, turning the bowl a bit and repeating the process. Be careful not to knock the air out of the mixture.

Divide the batter between the two greased cake pans. Bake for 15-18 minutes or just until the cake begins to brown and the edges begin to pull away from the pan. A gentle press of the fingers on the top should spring back. Let cool to room temperature before finishing or freezing.

Prepare the frosting and prepare to assemble:
Measure out the egg whites one at a time to be sure that no egg yolk is included. Place them into a very clean mixer bowl. Set it aside, ready to mix. In a medium-sized saucepan, mix the water, ¾ cup of sugar and the corn syrup. Start whipping the egg whites on high speed. On medium-high heat, bring the sugar syrup to a full boil. The moment the sugar syrup looks "foamy" across the entire surface, remove it from the heat and immediately drizzle it into the whipping egg whites. DO NOT scrape either the bowl or the pan. Let the mixture continue to whip until the outside of the mixer bowl is no longer warm to the touch. (To make cleanup easier, soak the syrup pan with hot water.)

MOCCA SPONGE CAKE cont.

Scrape the egg white mixture into a large bowl and set it aside. Without cleaning the mixer bowl, use it to whip the unsalted butter until it is light and fluffy. (Should the butter not be room temperature, melt 3 tablespoons of it, then whip.) Stir 1 teaspoon of Folger's Coffee Crystals into 2 tablespoons of strong coffee. Add this super strong coffee to the whipped butter and whip it in. Scrape the whipped butter mixture into the bowl with the egg white mixture and use a handheld wire whip to gently stir them together. In a small bowl, mix a ½ cup of coffee, 1 tablespoon of Folger's Coffee Crystals®, 2 tablespoons of sugar and the rum. Set it aside. Have a pastry brush handy. Remove the sponge cakes from the pans and rub any loose cake from around the edges. Clean and dry the cake pans. Use a serrated knife to carefully cut the cakes horizontally across the middle.

To assemble (see photo sequence, page 98):
Place a large dollop of the butter creme into each of the cake pans. Use a spatula to spread it over the bottom and all the way up the sides, being sure not to leave any "holes". **(A)** Place the top of one of the sponge cakes, cut side up, into the slathered pan. **(B)** Use the pastry brush to dab ¼ of the coffee/rum mixture over the cake half. Repeat the process for the second cake. Spoon additional butter creme onto the soaked cake halves **(C)** (leaving approximately 1 cup of frosting behind) and spread it evenly. **(D)** Invert the remaining cake halves on top of the spread butter creme in the cake pans, and dab the remaining coffee/rum mixture onto them. **(E)** Divide the remaining butter creme between the two cakes and spread over the bottom of each. **(F)** Place a baked meringue circle, flat side up, onto each and press lightly. **(G)** Cover each with a piece of plastic wrap. Freeze until hard. They can remain frozen for long periods of time.

To serve:
To remove a cake from the pan, dip the pan very briefly into a bowl of hot water and invert it. Press on one edge of the pan to push the cake out. As a last resort, use a knife to pry the cake out of the form, then use the same knife to patch any damage. Let it sit for 5-10 minutes to soften. Press the roasted almond slices around the outside. Shave chocolate curls on the top or drizzle with melted chocolate (See Chocolate for Topping Cakes). Decorate with purchased decorating flowers for a birthday or special occasion. Serve chilled or room temperature. To slice the cake, warm a knife by running hot water over the blade, then wipe it dry before cutting.

Délice

MOCCA SQUARES

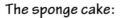

These are the Mocca Cake in the form of giant coffee-infused petit fours. Walter created the flavor using our regular brewed coffee boosted with Folger's coffee crystals. If the crystals are not in your pantry, simply brew a really strong cup of coffee or alternatively, just use the crystals in hot water to make the coffee.

You can bake the sponge cake ahead and freeze it until it is time to assemble everything, but the coffee butter creme does not store well and should be prepared fresh. It is very helpful to have the eggs and egg whites at room temperature, in order to maximize the volume increase when whipping them. Without leavening, it is the air that lifts the sponge cake.

Fondant, the traditional "icing" for petit fours is difficult to come by unless you are blessed with a specialty baking shop nearby. It must be used at just the correct temperature and can be very temperamental, so I have chosen to substitute a glaze recipe that has been modified from one of Gale Gand's (the Food Network). It can be used at room temperature and thickened with more powdered sugar or thinned using hot water, or in this case, coffee. If you don't need all the squares at once, dip as many as you need and freeze the layered cake and the fondant and dip more as needed.

Makes 24 or 30 squares.

Sponge Cake:
⅓ teaspoon butter
1 cup + 2 tablespoons cake or pastry flour
½ cup sugar
2 tablespoons vegetable oil
1 cup eggs (5 large eggs) – room temperature

Coffee Butter Creme:
½ cup egg whites (4 large eggs) – room temperature
¼ cup water
¾ cup + 1 tablespoon sugar, divided
1-½ teaspoons light corn syrup
13 tablespoons unsalted butter –
   room temperature is best
¼ cup + 2 tablespoons strong brewed coffee
2-½ teaspoons Folger's Coffee Crystals®, divided
1 tablespoon dark (gold) rum

2 tablespoons sliced, roasted almonds
   (see Roasted Almonds, page 42)

Coffee flavored Glaze:
⅔ cup light corn syrup
⅔ cup hot brewed coffee
7 cups powdered sugar

The sponge cake:
Preheat oven all the way to 350°.

Cut a piece of parchment to fit the bottom of a 9 x 13 inch baking pan. Set the parchment piece aside. Melt the ⅓ teaspoon of butter and use it to grease the baking pan. Place the cut piece of parchment into the bottom of the greased pan.

Measure, sift and set aside the flour. Measure and set aside the sugar and then the oil. Open the eggs into a mixer bowl and begin whipping them at medium speed. Add the sugar to the whipping eggs. Once the sugar is in, turn the mixer up to high speed and let it run for 5-7 minutes. The mixture will increase in volume considerably and become a pale yellow. Use a rubber spatula to gently fold the flour in by hand. Next, add the oil. Gently fold it in with the rubber spatula by lifting it from the bottom of the bowl, folding it over, turning the bowl a bit and repeating the process. Be careful not to knock the air out of the mixture.

Pour the batter into the greased, paper-lined baking pan. Bake for 15-18 minutes or just until the cake begins to brown and the edges begin to pull away from the pan. A gentle press of the fingers on the cake top should spring back. Let cool to room temperature before finishing or freezing.

Prepare the frosting and prepare to assemble:
Measure out the egg whites one at a time to be sure that no egg yolk is included. Place them into a very clean mixer bowl. Set them aside, ready to mix. In a medium-sized saucepan, mix the water, ¾ cup of sugar and the corn syrup. Start whipping the egg whites on high speed. On medium-high heat, bring the sugar syrup to a full boil. The moment the sugar syrup looks "foamy" across the entire surface, remove it from the heat and immediately drizzle it into the whipping egg whites. DO NOT scrape either the bowl or the pan. Let the mixture continue to whip until the outside of the mixer bowl is no longer warm to the touch. (To make cleanup easier, soak the syrup pan with hot water.)

Délice

Scrape the egg white mixture into a large bowl and set it aside. Without cleaning the mixer bowl, use it to whip the unsalted butter until it is light and fluffy. (Should the butter not be room temperature, melt 3 tablespoons of it, then whip it.) Stir 1 teaspoon of Folger's Coffee Crystals into 2 tablespoons of strong coffee. Add this super strong coffee to the whipped butter and whip it in. Scrape the whipped butter mixture into the bowl with the egg white mixture and use a handheld wire whip to gently stir them together. Set the mixture aside.

In a small bowl, mix ¼ cup of coffee, 1-½ teaspoons of Folger's Coffee Crystals®, 1 tablespoon of sugar and the rum. Set it aside. Have a pastry brush handy. Remove the sponge cake from the pan by carefully inverting it onto a cutting board. Clean and dry the baking pan. Peel the parchment from the baked cake and discard it. Use a serrated knife to carefully cut the cake horizontally through the middle, creating two layers. **(A)+(B)**

To assemble:

Cut a piece of parchment so that it is the length of the baking pan, but that extends above the sides. (This will make it easier to remove the cake squares later.) Place half of the butter creme into the paper-lined pan. Spread the creme over the bottom. Gently turn the top layer of sponge cake upside down and place it into the pan, on top of the butter creme. If it breaks, just fit the pieces in. Use the pastry brush to dab all of the coffee/rum mixture over the cake in the pan. Scrape the remaining butter creme onto the coffee-infused cake in the pan and spread it evenly. Invert the remaining cake layer and place it on top of the spread butter creme in the pan. Gently press it down. Cover the exposed cake with plastic wrap. Freeze until hard (several hours or overnight).

Coating the cake squares:

Prepare the glaze in a large bowl, by using a wire whip to stir the corn syrup into the hot coffee until it is dissolved. Continuing to use the wire whip, stir the powdered sugar in until smooth. Pour a portion of the glaze into a steeply sided container so that it will be deep enough to dip the cake squares into. Set the glaze aside. Place a wire rack over a pan to catch the glaze as it drips off of the cake squares. Set it aside.

Remove the plastic covering from the frozen cake. Pull a metal spatula or knife between the cake and the pan where the two touch. Gently remove the cake from the pan by inverting it onto a cutting board. Peel the parchment away and discard it. Cut the cake into roughly 2 inch squares. **(C)** Have the roasted almonds and a fork handy.

Dip each cake square into the glaze, using the fork underneath the "top" of the square to help lift it out. Hold the square over the bowl momentarily before placing it onto the wire rack to allow some of the glaze to run off. Refill the glaze as needed. It is important that the cake squares be frozen; if the butter creme becomes too warm, place the cake pieces back into the freezer momentarily before continuing to dip them. The glaze acts as a protective coating for the cake so it may be necessary to use a small spatula or knife to spread it over bare spots. Any glaze leftover once the squares have been dipped once should be spooned or ladled over the squares for a second "coat". Place several roasted almond slices in the middle of each dipped square for decoration. **(D)** Refrigerate, or better, freeze the squares, on the rack if possible, before placing them into air-tight containers or serving them chilled.

The glaze that drips into the pan underneath the wire rack can be scraped into a container and frozen for future use.

A

B

C

D

CHOCOLATE BUTTER CREME SPONGE CAKE

This cake was not offered out of the freezer case for a number of years, except during the holiday season, when it took the form of Büche de Noel. Melted bittersweet chocolate flavors the butter creme, which is layered with a light chocolate sponge cake.

There are a number of steps involved in getting a complete cake. I have found it helpful to bake the meringue bases a day ahead. You can even bake the sponge cakes ahead and freeze them until it is time to assemble everything. I have been true to the process that we used, but should you need the cake soon after assembly, reverse the assembly process without the cake pan. Begin with the meringue on the bottom and layer as you would any other cake.

It is very helpful to have the eggs and egg whites at room temperature, in order to maximize the volume increase when whipping them. Without leavening, it is the air that lifts the sponge cake.

Makes two 8-inch cakes.

Use Baked Meringue with Almond recipe (page 83) to create two 8-inch circle bases.

Chocolate Sponge Cake:
½ teaspoon butter
1 cup cake or pastry flour
3 tablespoons cocoa powder
½ cup sugar
2 tablespoons vegetable oil
1 cup eggs (5 large eggs) – room temperature

Chocolate Butter Creme:
½ cup egg whites (4 large eggs)
¼ cup water
1-½ teaspoon light corn syrup
¾ cup sugar
13 tablespoons unsalted butter –
   room temperature is best
6 ounces bittersweet or semi-sweet chocolate

Milk chocolate to shave or drizzle on top (see Chocolate for Topping Cakes, page 99).

The sponge cake:
Preheat oven all the way to 350°.

Melt the ½ teaspoon of butter and use it to grease two 8-inch round cake pans. Measure and sift together the flour and the cocoa powder. Set them aside. Measure and set aside the sugar and then the oil. Begin whipping the eggs at medium speed. Add the sugar to the eggs. Once the sugar is in, turn the mixer up to high speed and let it go for 5-7 minutes. Use a rubber spatula to gently fold the flour in by hand. Next, add the oil. Fold it in by lifting it from the bottom of the bowl, folding it over, turning the bowl a bit and repeating the process. Be careful not to knock the air out of the mixture.

Divide the batter between the two greased cake pans. Bake for 15-20 minutes or just until the cake begins to brown and the edges begin to pull away from the pan. A gentle press of the fingers on the top should spring back. Let cool to room temperature before finishing or freezing.

Prepare the frosting and prepare to assemble:
Measure out the egg whites one at a time to be sure that no egg yolk is included. Place them into a very clean mixer bowl. Set it aside, ready to mix. In a medium-sized saucepan, mix the water, ¾ cup of sugar and the corn syrup. Start whipping the egg whites on high speed. On medium-high heat, bring the sugar syrup to a full boil. The moment the sugar syrup looks "foamy" across the entire surface, remove it from the heat and immediately drizzle it into the whipping egg whites. DO NOT scrape either the bowl or the pan. Let the mixture continue to whip until the outside of the mixer bowl is no longer warm to the touch. (To make cleanup easier, soak the syrup pan with hot water.)

Scrape the egg white mixture into a large bowl and set it aside. Without cleaning the mixer bowl, use it to whip the unsalted butter until it is light and fluffy. (Should the butter not be room temperature, melt 3 tablespoons of it, then whip.) While the butter is whipping, melt the chocolate by using a double-boiler over low-medium heat or microwaving it, then stirring it, in 5-10 second intervals. Add the melted chocolate to the whipped butter and mix. Scrape the whipped butter mixture into the bowl with the egg white mixture and use a handheld wire whip to gently stir them together. Remove the sponge cakes from the pans and rub any loose cake from around the edges. Clean and dry the cake pans. Use a serrated knife to carefully cut the cakes horizontally across the middle.

To assemble (see photo sequence, page 98):

Place a large dollop of the butter creme into each of the cake pans. Use a spatula to spread it over the bottom and all the way up the sides, being sure not to leave any "holes". **(A)** Place the top of one of the sponge cakes, cut side up, into the slathered pan. **(B)** Repeat the process for the second cake. Spoon additional butter creme onto the cake halves **(C)** (leaving approximately 1 cup of frosting behind) and spread it evenly. **(D)** Invert the remaining cake halves on top of the spread butter creme in the cake pans. **(E)** Divide the remaining butter creme between the two cakes and spread over the bottom of each. **(F)** Place a baked meringue circle, flat side up, onto each and press lightly. **(G)** Cover each with a piece of plastic wrap. Freeze until hard. They can remain frozen for long periods of time.

To serve:

To remove a cake from the pan, dip the pan very briefly into a bowl of hot water and invert it. Press on one edge of the pan to push the cake out. As a last resort, use a knife to pry the cake out of the form, then use the same knife to patch any damage. Shave chocolate curls on the top or drizzle with melted chocolate (See Chocolate for Topping Cakes). Decorate with purchased decorating flowers for a birthday or special occasion. Serve chilled or room temperature. To slice the cake, warm a knife by running hot water over the blade, then wipe it dry before cutting.

Walter's surprise 75th birthday party

Walter and grandaughter, Erica,
assembling a gingerbread house

Délice

Gingerbread

Author with niece, Erica, creating gingerbread house parts

GINGERBREAD COOKIES

The secret to this recipe, and several similar ones, were the "goodies". This was our euphemism for all the old or broken pastries that we collected in the freezer. Nothing that had sugar or butter in it ever went to waste; a concept that is now foreign to modern food service. Also, we used a leavening agent called ammonium carbonate, which is imported from Great Britain and seems available only as a wholesale item. Honestly, this recipe was the most challenging of all the pastry recipes to try to get a flavor and texture true to the product that we sold.

Makes 8-9 (5-½ inch tall) gingerbreaad people or 20-25 (2-½ inch) cookies.

Prepare an eggwash (see Glossary) and refrigerate.

4 ounces (16 - 1-¾ inch) ginger snap cookies
½ cup + 2 tablespoons + 1 teaspoon milk, divided
3 cups cake flour
5 teaspoons ground cinnamon
¾ teaspoon baking soda
5 tablespoons butter
½ teaspoon lemon zest (see Glossary)
½ teaspoon vanilla
½ cup honey
5 tablespoons sugar

Soak the cookies in ½ cup + 2 tablespoons of the milk for a few minutes. In a large mixing bowl, assemble the flour, the cinnamon, and the soda. Set them aside. Melt the butter and mix it into the cookie "mash", along with the lemon zest and the vanilla. Set it aside. Measure the honey and the sugar into a small saucepan and set aside briefly. Add the cookie "mash" to the dry ingredients and mix briefly. Heat the honey/sugar over medium heat just until it begins to boil. Add the honey/sugar to the rest of the ingredients and stir until well mixed. Scrape the dough into a small bowl and let it cool to room temperature before covering it and placing in the refrigerator for several hours or overnight. It is helpful to take the dough out and let it sit at room temperature for 30 minutes before rolling it.

Preheat oven to 375°.

Put a teaspoon of milk into a small bowl. Set it aside. Have a pastry brush handy. Line one or two baking sheets with parchment paper. Flour a rolling surface and scrape the dough out onto it. It will be fairly stiff, so knead it briefly to "loosen" it up a bit. Shape it into a log and then use a rolling pin to roll it until it is roughly ¼ inch thick. Dust the surface of the dough and the rolling surface with flour as needed to keep it from sticking.

Use the cookie cutters of your choice to cut as many cookies as possible. Place them onto the lined baking sheets with enough room between them to expand. Ball up the leftover dough and roll it out and cut more cookies. Repeat the process until the dough is too small to cut another cookie.

Brush each cookie with milk. Bake for 20-25 minutes or until the cookies begin to brown around the edges. Immediately after removing the tray from the oven, brush each cookie with the eggwash. This creates a shine.

Decorate the cookies using Royal Frosting (page 46). **(A)** For a special look, dip each cookie quickly into colored sprinkles immediately after the frosting is applied. **(B)**

A

B

GINGERBREAD HOUSE

The week following Thanksgiving was always Gingerbread House week. In early November we would have ordered little santas from a catalog. On Monday or Tuesday Walter would stir up a huge batch of gingerbread dough. As time allowed, we would make the Cornet chimneys, the Meringue Mushrooms, and the chocolate "leaves". On the designated afternoon, about the time we closed the doors for the day, the entire family would gather at the shop. For the rest of the afternoon and well into the evening, we would bake and then assemble 12 to 20 Gingerbread Houses. There are two options with Gingerbread Houses; eat them (with the help of milk, coffee or hot chocolate to dip in) or keep them. One of our customers has a gingerbread house that is 30 years old.

Organizing all the pieces and parts for a Gingerbread House is what takes the most time. The actual assembly can take as little as 15 minutes. I have included all of the little things that would have been on one of our houses, but please keep in mind that this is a creative endeavor. As such, you can invest as much or as little energy as you have time for. The Meringue Mushrooms, which must be made ahead of time, will result in extra meringues and are very fragile. Consider doing without them, or purchase commercial meringues and assemble them as you would home-baked ones. They will still resemble mushrooms. The Cornet recipe (page 73) was used to make the chimneys, but I strongly urge the substitution of an ordinary sugar cone (the kind used to serve ice cream in.) The gingerbread pieces can actually be baked several weeks ahead, cooled, layered between parchment paper and frozen until needed.

Makes one A-frame gingerbread house (10 inches tall) on a circular base.

Create the patterns for the house pieces and base using paper, or preferably, cardboard (see Gingerbread House Pattern, page 117).

Prepare Meringue Mushrooms (page 83), but do not assemble, or purchase baked meringue "kisses".

Prepare 2 batches of Gingerbread Cookie dough (page 112). Refrigerate.

Prepare a couple of Cornets (page 73) for a chimney (one extra in case of breakage), or purchase a sugar cone.

1-½ ounces milk chocolate coating, chocolate chips or green chocolate

1 egg

2 teaspoons milk

cookie cutters: tree, star + 2 others of your choice

cookie cutters: 1 inch scalloped circle, 1-½ inch scalloped circle (optional)

pastry bag with 1 small round and 1 large star decorating tips

1, 2 or 3 colors of nonpareils or sprinkles of your choice (optional)

1 santa (1-½ - 3 inches tall)

1 large cotton ball

Royal Frosting:
3-¾ cups (1 pound) powdered sugar
6 tablespoons egg white (3 eggs)
1-½ teaspoons cream of tartar
1-½ teaspoons clear vanilla (optional)

Chocolate leaves:
Line a tray or baking sheet with parchment. Melt the chocolate by using a double-boiler over low-medium heat or microwaving it, then stirring it, in 5-10 second intervals. Put the melted chocolate into a pastry bag with a small round tip or into a small plastic food baggie then just barely cut one corner off. Pipe the chocolate into the shape of a leaf onto the parchment by making a very close zigzag pattern approximately 2 inches long, giving it a point, then making the same zigzag pattern down the other side of where the "stem" would be. **(A)** Be sure that the patterns touch at the "stem". Use all the chocolate to make leaves. Refrigerate or freeze until needed.

continued on next page...

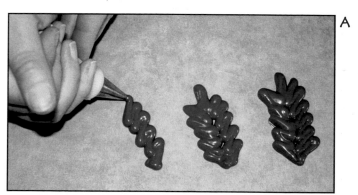

A

Rolling and baking the gingerbread:

Preheat oven to 375°.

It is helpful to take the gingerbread dough out and let it sit at room temperature for at least 30 minutes before rolling it. Prepare an eggwash by using a fork to whip the egg. Set it aside. Put the two teaspoons of milk into a small bowl. Set it aside. Have a pastry brush (or two) handy. Line two, perhaps three, baking sheets with parchment paper.

Flour a rolling surface and scrape one batch of the gingerbread dough out onto it. It will be fairly stiff, so knead it briefly to "loosen" it up. Shape it into a log and then use a rolling pin to roll it until it is roughly ¼ inch thick. Dust the surface of the dough and the rolling surface with flour as needed to keep it from sticking. Place the pattern for the circular Base on top of the dough. Use a jagger (see Glossary), pizza cutter or knife to cut around the pattern. Place the large circle onto one of the baking sheets. Place the pattern over it to check its shape. Brush each cut-out piece of dough lightly with milk.

If you are a multitasker, place the Base in the oven while you are cutting out the other pieces. Bake for 15-20 minutes or until the dough begins to brown around the edges and a bit across the top surface. Brush each piece of gingerbread with eggwash immediately after taking it from the oven. (Do not try to remove the pieces from the parchment until they are room temperature.) As a baking sheet fills up, go ahead and bake it if your confidence and oven space allow. The other choice is cut all the pieces out, then bake them.

Add the leftover rolled gingerbread dough to the second batch of dough and knead them together. Roll all of it out until it is again ¼ inch thick. Use the house side pattern, Side A to cut out one side. Remove the pattern and place Side A onto one of the baking sheets. Use the pattern to check its shape on the sheet. Use the cookie cutter of your choice (not a tree or a star) to cut a cookie out of Side A, with the bottom of the cookie cutter centered and approximately 2 inches from the bottom edge. Place the resulting cookie onto the baking sheet. Also cut a 1-½ inch hole in the upper right-hand

corner of Side A, with the center roughly 2 inches in from the top edge and the right edge. (Don't have a round cookie cutter? Use a small drinking glass.) This is where the chimney will fit. (Set aside the bit of circular dough and add it back into the rest of the dough with your next roll.) Brush Side A and the cookie lightly with milk.

Whenever there is no longer sufficient rolled dough to cut pieces out, wad the gingerbread dough up and roll it out again.

Flip the house side pattern over and cut Side B out of the rolled dough. Remove the pattern and place Side B onto a baking sheet. Use the pattern to check its shape. Use a different cookie cutter of your choice (not a tree or a star) to cut a cookie from Side B. Place the resulting cookie onto the baking sheet. Brush Side B and the cookie lightly with milk.

Use the pattern to cut out the house Front. Remove the pattern and place the house Front onto a baking sheet. Use a knife to cut a 2 inch door out of the bottom edge. Use the pattern to check its shape. Place the door onto the baking sheet. Cut one house Back using the pattern. Remove the pattern and place the house Back onto a baking sheet. Cut a 1 inch hole in the back for a window, centered and approximately 3 inches from the bottom edge. (Set aside the bit of circular dough and add it back into the rest of the dough with your next roll.) Use the pattern to check its shape. Brush the Front, the Back and the door lightly with milk. Use the remaining gingerbread dough to cut out a star and as many as 4 trees. After that, any remainder is a bonus. Make gingerbread cookies out of it or freeze it for future cookies. Place the star, trees and any extra cookies onto the baking sheets. Brush with milk.

When the baking is all done, you should have the circular Base, the two house Sides, the house Front and Back, the two cookies cut from the house Sides, a door, a star and 1-4 trees.

Royal Frosting:

Whip the powdered sugar, the egg whites and the cream of tartar 2-4 minutes until very white and fluffy. Ideally you want the frosting thick enough that it will hold a peak, but light enough to easily squeeze from a pastry tube or plastic bag. Adjust the consistency by using drops of water or tiny portions of egg white to thin it or adjust it the other way by adding one tablespoon of powdered sugar at a time. While decorating, keep your mixing bowl covered with plastic or a damp towel to keep the royal from drying prematurely.

Prepare to assemble:

Assemble the Meringue Mushrooms according to the recipe. Set them aside. Organize a pastry bag with a small round tip. Fill it with frosting. Set it aside with the tip up against a damp cloth. If using sprinkles, pour each color into a pie pan or onto a plate. One at a time, decorate the star, the two side cookies, the door, and the tree(s) by first using the round-tipped pastry bag to pipe a pattern onto the cookie, then gently dipping the frosted side of the cookie into the sprinkles. Have the santa, a chimney and the chocolate leaves handy.

Assembly:

Place the circular Base onto something that will keep it rigid, such as a cardboard cake circle or a large, flat plate. If during the assembly process, a piece should break, use frosting to glue it back together. Later, decorate over the seam. Change the tip on the pastry bag to a large star tip. Use it to pipe royal down the left edge of the house Front (looking at the shiny side of the gingerbread). Put the pastry bag down. Holding the house Front in your right hand and Side A (the one with the chimney hole) in your left hand, place the two pieces onto the base, with the Front so that it will fit just "inside" the sides. **(A)** Lean Side A over onto the frosted edge. If you have an extra set of hands helping, have them hold the two pieces. Otherwise, you must let it balance while you pipe frosting onto the right edge of the house Back. Position it at the very back of Side A, but also so that it will fit "inside" the two sides. **(B)** Pipe frosting up the exposed edge of the house front, across the top edge of Side A and back down the exposed edge of the house Back. **(C)** Position Side B over the frosted edges. **(D)** Making small, careful adjustments, position the front and back so that they are not too "sunken". Also position the house on the base to maximize the space in front and minimize the space at the back.

Use the star-tipped pastry bag to pipe frosting in a line where the house meets the base, in the front and the back. Once hard, this will hold the house in place.

continued on next page...

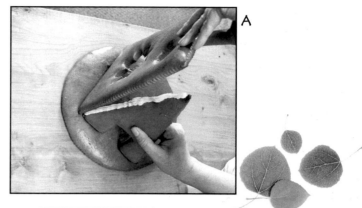

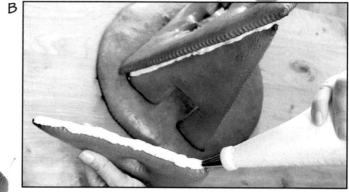

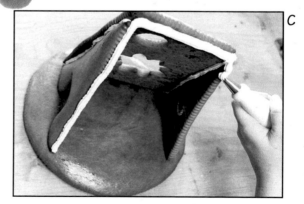

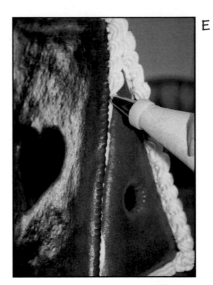

E

Decorating:

Use the frosting filled pastry bag with the star tip to pipe a circular, overlapping border across the top of the house. Use a scalloped border or stars to cover the four exposed side edges, two in front and two in back. **(E)** Pipe around the little window on the back and around the doorway on the front.

Using frosting as "glue", place the star at the top of the Front. You may have to hold it in place briefly. Glue the door, decorated side out, to one side of the doorway. Glue santa in the doorway. On Side B, outline the cookie "window" with royal and place the appropriate cookie back over the opening. Run a line of frosting where the house meets the base. Glue a couple of the chocolate leaves and a tree or two up against the house. If you have mushrooms, glue two of them near the house. On Side A, glue the appropriate cookie back over the opening and place chocolate leaves and a tree or two against the house. **(F)** Use a dab of frosting to glue a cotton ball into the chimney. Gently tug the cotton into a shape resembling smoke. Outline the chimney hole with a generous amount of frosting. Carefully position the chimney in the hole. Using a circular, overlapping or scalloped border, outline the upper outside edge of the circular Base. **(G)**

F

Squeeze the royal from the pastry tube back into the mixing bowl with any leftover frosting. Color this remaining frosting with a drop or two of the food coloring of your choice and put it back into the pastry tube. Use the round decorating tip to decorate the open spaces of the sides and front of the house as you see fit.

Leave the house out to harden.

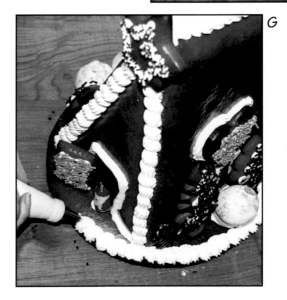

G

GINGERBREAD HOUSE PATTERN

Copy or trace the 3 patterns
labeled Side A, Front and
Back. Cut them out of paper
or cardboard. Label the back
side of Side A, Side B.

For the circular Base create a
pattern for a circle that is 10
inches across.

SIDE A

10 inches

8 7/8 inches

7 3/4 inches

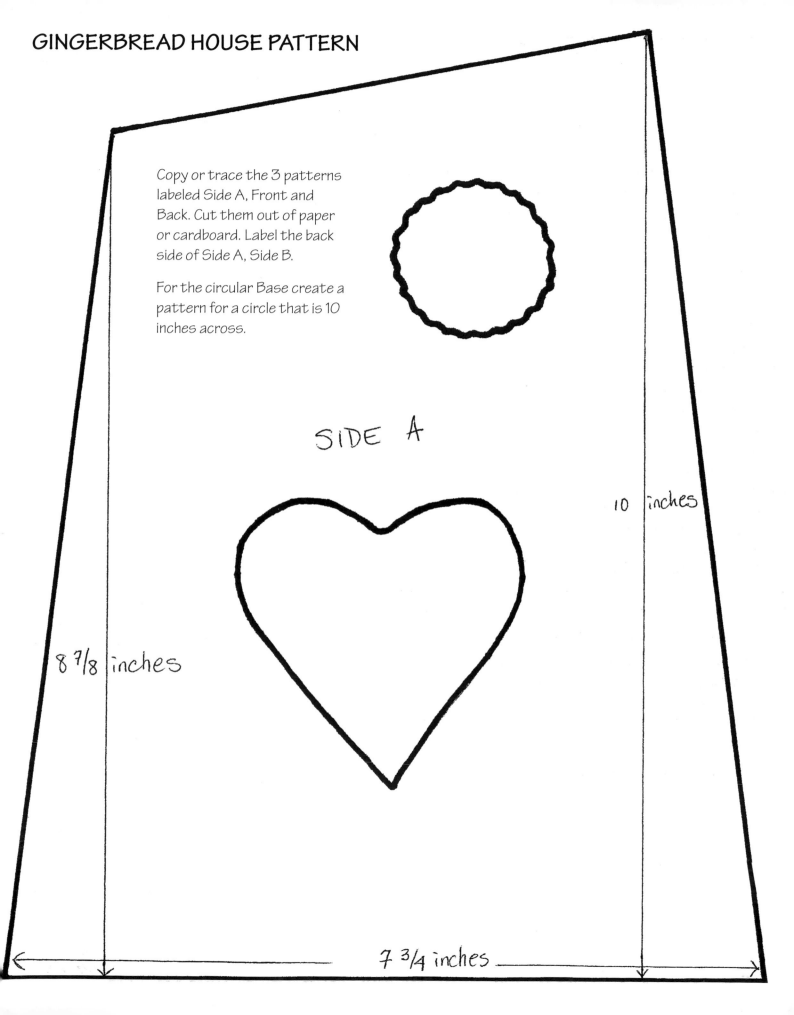

GINGERBREAD HOUSE PATTERN

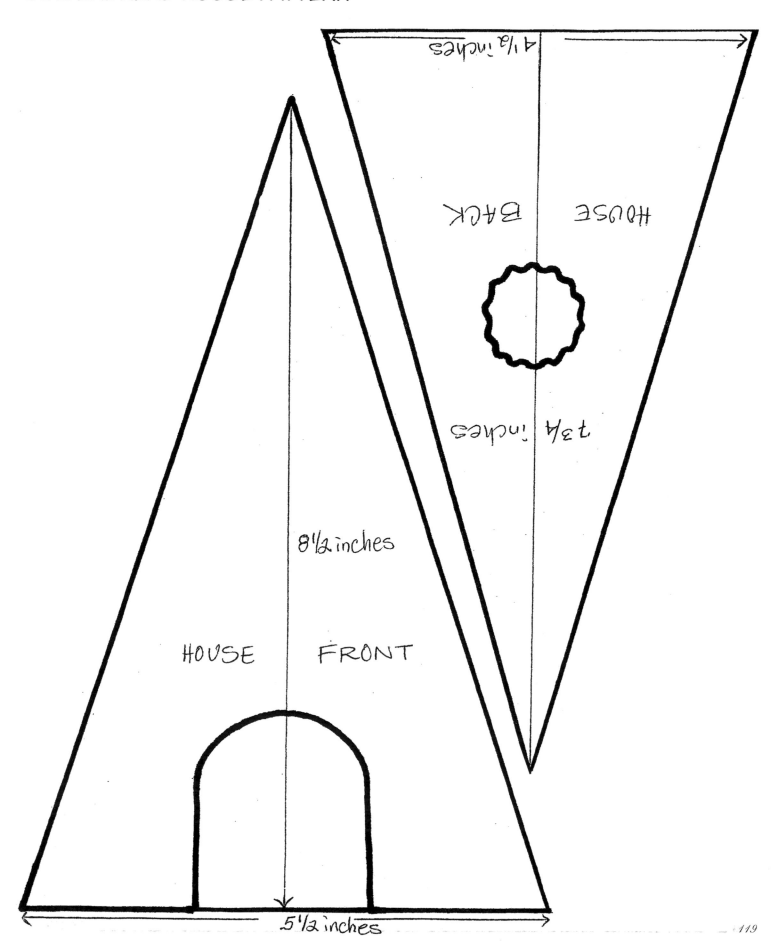

4½ inches

BACK   HOUSE

1¾ inches

8½ inches

HOUSE   FRONT

5½ inches

PRESERVES

What is the difference between jam and jelly? Jam has the whole fruit in it; jelly is made from just the juice.

I believe that people don't make homemade jam or jelly because there is a preconceived notion that it is very time consuming. Making preserves in small batches actually takes very little time, it is juicing wild berries that does. We made a number of our preserves from frozen or even canned fruits, which cut down on prep time considerably. Don't get me wrong, I believe that there is something very elemental in picking berries in the fall and we all have strong memories of the distinctive smell of boiling rosehips.

I encourage you to give at least one recipe a try. You will be reluctant to purchase preserves at the store afterward.

PROCESSING WILD BERRIES FOR JELLY

Once the fun part of picking wild berries is done, it is time to process them. The berries can be frozen whole for long periods of time, or you can process them and freeze the juice in re-used plastic milk or juice jugs. Experience taught me to measure the juice and label the amount on the container before freezing. It doesn't hurt to add a bit of water in order to make the quantities even cupsful before freezing. Be aware that many wild berries are what the Native Americans used as dye and that the juice can stain clothing and surfaces.

Place the fresh or frozen berries into a large stockpot and cover with water. Leaving the stockpot uncovered, bring the whole to a boil. Lower the heat to keep it simmering for an hour or so. You may have to add water to keep the berries covered. Remove from heat and let cool to a workable temperature. It is okay to refrigerate the juice and/or the berries overnight anywhere during this process if you do not have the time to do every step in one day.

Use a potato masher to mash the berries in the water. Place a collander into a large bowl and drape a large square of multi-layered cheesecloth into the collander. Have another large bowl or container ready to hand. Scoop a reasonable amount of the berries and water into the cheesecloth. Bring the four corners of cheesecloth together and twist and squeeze. Place the squeezed contents of the cheesecloth into the extra bowl. Repeat the process for all of the cooked berries and pour any remaining stockpot contents through the cheesecloth to remove any leaves or other debris.

To get every last drop from the berries, put the balls of squeezed berries back into the stockpot, cover them with water and boil them a second time. Repeat the cheesecloth procedure, but discard the berries this time. Mix the juices from the first and second squeezings. Measure and pour into containers to freeze or make into jelly the same day. If you intend to freeze the juice, do not fill the containers all the way full as the juice will expand when frozen.

Halloween 1988

APPLE BUTTER

Several apple trees around the New Castle home often provide bucketsfull of fruit and canning has become a fall ritual. This is one of those foods that people are passionate about – either they absolutely love it or they hate it. The original recipe came out of Rombauers' The Joy of Cooking, but Viola has modified it over the years. The newer reprintings of the cookbook no longer even have the recipe. Another tradition gone by the wayside.

The preparation of all the apples can be quite time consuming and our modern lifestyles rarely include much spare time, so, if picking apples and cooking them down for applesauce is unrealistic for you, purchase applesauce from the grocery store. Be sure that it is a "no sugar added" version, without any salt.

Core and quarter apples and cook slowly in water. Work cooked fruit through a food mill. (Omit if using purchased applesauce.)

For each cupful of prepared or purchased applesauce:
½ cup sugar
1 teaspoon ground cinnamon
½ teaspoon ground clove
¼ teaspoon allspice

Measure the prepared or purchased applesauce into a stockpot or large saucepan. Add the sugar and spices. Cook the mixture over low-medium heat, stirring very often, until it boils even when stirred. Place a small quantity on a plate. When no rim of liquid separates around the edge of the apple butter on the plate, it is done. Keep in mind that the smaller the amount of apple butter, the less time this will take.

To actually seal the jars of apple butter, bring a stockpot full of water to a rolling boil. Very carefully place empty canning jars with the lids separate into the boiling water and wait until it boils again. Carefully remove one jar at a time and fill with hot apple butter, wipe the rim of the jar clean and screw the lid on. Set these aside on a heat resistant surface or towel. As the apple butter cools the lids should "pop" as the lids are sucked down. Any that don't seal should be refrigerated and eaten first.

APRICOT JAM

For a very long time we did this the hard way – purchased fresh apricots when in season, cut them in half, pitted them and froze them by the bagful. Then, in mid-winter one year, we ran out of the frozen apricots and had to come up with an alternative, since this was a jam that we actually used to make several of the pastries. Much to our surprise the flavor was just as good, and some of the customers felt it was actually better.

Makes 3-½ pints.

15.25 ounce can apricot halves in heavy syrup
   (1-½ cups)
11.5 ounce can apricot nectar
   (peach is a good substitute)
1 tablespoon light corn syrup
3-½ cups sugar
1 package Sure-Jell® Premium Fruit Pectin - labeled
   "For Less or No Sugar Recipes"

Measure the sugar. In a small bowl, mix ¼ cup of the measured sugar with the contents of the Sure-Jell® packet and set aside. Pour the apricots with the juice from the can into a small stockpot. Add the nectar and the corn syrup (which prevents the sugar from recrystalizing later.) Use a wire whip to mix the pectin mixture into the apricot. Bring the mixture to a full boil and quickly add and stir in the remaining sugar. Bring the whole to a full boil once again and boil for one minute. Remove from the heat.

Health food codes prevented us from actually sealing our jars of jam and jelly. So, they required refrigeration and had a finite shelf life. If you intend simply to refrigerate the jelly, ladle it into room temperature jars (very cold jars might crack). Let the jam reach room temperature completely, even so far as to leave them out overnight, before putting lids on. If you wish to actually seal the jars of jam for non-refrigerated storage, follow the instructions included with the Sure-Jell®.

BLUEBERRY JAM

Blueberries offer a lengthy list of health benefits, as do most berries. I would offer one warning about making this jam; the native americans used these berries to dye cloth and that is what will happen if you should splash any of the juice onto your own clothing. It stains.

Makes 3-½ pints.

2 pounds blueberries (7 cups frozen)
1-½ cups water
4 cups sugar
1 tablespoon light corn syrup
1 package Sure-Jell® Premium Fruit Pectin - labeled "For Less or No Sugar Recipes"

Measure the sugar. In a small bowl, mix ¼ cup of the measured sugar with the contents of the Sure-Jell® packet. In a stockpot, mix the blueberries, water and corn syrup. If the blueberries are frozen, heat the mixture until they thaw. Stir the pectin/sugar into the blueberries. Bring the resulting mixture to a full rolling boil, stirring very often. Stir the remaining sugar in quickly and let the mixture reach a rolling boil once again. Boil for 1 minute and remove from heat.

Health food codes prevented us from actually sealing our jars of jam and jelly. So, they required refrigeration and had a finite shelf life. If you intend simply to refrigerate the jelly, ladle it into room temperature jars (very cold jars might crack). Let the jam reach room temperature completely, even so far as to leave them out overnight, before putting lids on. If you wish to actually seal the jars of jam for non-refrigerated storage, follow the instructions included with the Sure-Jell®.

CHOKECHERRY JELLY

Chokecherry bushes grow all over Colorado, but seem to prefer areas near water. In the spring the ends of the branches are covered with the bottlebrush clusters of small white flowers. Later, as the fruit ripen, they hang in small bunches, looking a bit like very small round purple grapes. The birds and bears just love them, but for people to eat them raw can cause quite a pucker (be sure to spit the seed out). Once they are cooked up they are much sweeter. As with any wild berry picking, do your research or consult someone who knows what they are doing to be sure you are picking from the right bushes and leave plenty on the bush for all the critters that depend on the food to survive.

Makes 3-½ pints.

4 cups chokecherry juice (see Processing Wild Berries, page 121)
1 tablespoon light corn syrup
4 cups sugar
1 package Sure-Jell® Premium Fruit Pectin - labeled "For Less or No Sugar Recipes"

Measure the sugar. In a small bowl, mix ¼ cup of the measured sugar with the contents of the Sure-Jell® packet. In a stockpot, use a wire whip to stir together the chokecherry juice, corn syrup and the pectin mixture. Bring the resulting mixture to a full rolling boil, stirring very often. Stir the remaining sugar in quickly and let the mixture reach a rolling boil once again. Boil for 1 minute and remove from heat.

Health food codes prevented us from actually sealing our jars of jam and jelly. If you intend simply to refrigerate the jelly, ladle it into room temperature jars (very cold jars might crack). Let the jelly reach room temperature completely, even so far as to leave them out overnight, before putting lids on. If you wish to actually seal the jars of jelly for non-refrigerated storage, follow the instructions included with the Sure-Jell®.

Délice

CURRANT JELLY

The several different varieties of wild currant growing in the Rocky Mountains are in the same family of plants as gooseberries. Pick wild currants only with the advice of a truly knowledgeable person. It is better to find someone with a currant bush in his or her yard and ask their permission to pick the berries. Give them a small jar of the jelly when you are done. Better yet, plant a bush in your back yard. Birds love them.

Makes 3-½ pints.

4 cups currant juice (see Processing Wild Berries, page 121)
1 tablespoon light corn syrup
4 cups sugar
1 package Sure-Jell® Premium Fruit Pectin - labeled "For Less or No Sugar Recipes"

Measure the sugar. In a small bowl, mix ¼ cup of the measured sugar with the contents of the Sure-Jell® packet. In a stockpot, use a wire whip to stir together the currant juice, corn syrup and the pectin mixture. Bring the resulting mixture to a full rolling boil, stirring very often. Stir the remaining sugar in quickly and let the mixture reach a rolling boil once again. Boil for 1 minute and remove from heat.

Health food codes prevented us from actually sealing our jars of jam and jelly. If you intend simply to refrigerate the jelly, ladle it into room temperature jars (very cold jars might crack). Let the jelly reach room temperature completely, even so far as to leave them out overnight, before putting lids on. If you wish to actually seal the jars of jelly for non-refrigerated storage, follow the instructions included with the Sure-Jell®.

RASPBERRY JAM

We made a variety of jams over the years, but we inevitably sold more of the raspberry than all the others combined. We used it to fill the Viennese Wafers, the Linzer Torte, and the Shells. It served as the topping for our cheesecakes and is my personal favorite on warm Holiday Butter and Egg Bread.

Makes 3-½ pints.

24 ounces (1-½ pounds) raspberries (fresh or frozen)
2 cups water
1 tablespoon light corn syrup
4 cups sugar
1 package Sure-Jell® Premium Fruit Pectin – labeled "For Less or No Sugar Recipes"

Measure the sugar. In a small bowl, mix ¼ cup of the measured sugar with the contents of the Sure-Jell® packet. In a stockpot, mix the berries, water and corn syrup. If the berries are frozen, heat the mixture until they thaw. Stir the pectin/sugar into the berries. Bring the resulting mixture to a full rolling boil, stirring very often. Stir the remaining sugar in quickly and let the mixture reach a rolling boil once again. Boil for 1 minute and remove from heat.

Health food codes prevented us from actually sealing our jars of jam and jelly. So, they required refrigeration and had a finite shelf life. If you intend simply to refrigerate the jelly, let it sit for 15-30 minutes then ladle it into room temperature jars (very cold jars might crack). Let the jam reach room temperature completely, even so far as to leave them out overnight, before putting lids on. If you wish to actually seal the jars of jam for non-refrigerated storage, follow the instructions included with the Sure-Jell®.

ROSE HIP JELLY

A rose hip is the fruit that is the result of a pollinated rose. Native rose bushes grow all along the bike paths and creeks of Colorado. Picking rose hips in the fall became a harvest ritual for my husband and I. At the elevations that we usually picked them, they would ripen as the Aspen leaves were changing colors. We received some odd looks from archery hunters through the years. Please remember the wildlife that depend on these wild berries for their survival and leave lots of the hips on the bushes.

Makes 3-½ pints.

4 cups rose hip juice (see Processing Wild Berries, page 121)
1 tablespoon light corn syrup
4 cups sugar
1 package Sure-Jell® Premium Fruit Pectin - labeled "For Less or No Sugar Recipes"

Measure the sugar. In a small bowl, mix ¼ cup of the measured sugar with the contents of the Sure-Jell® packet. In a stockpot, use a wire whip to stir together the rose hip juice, corn syrup and the pectin mixture. Bring the resulting mixture to a full rolling boil, stirring very often. Stir the remaining sugar in quickly and let the mixture reach a rolling boil once again. Boil for 1 minute and remove from heat.

Health food codes prevented us from actually sealing our jars of jam and jelly. So, they required refrigeration and had a finite shelf life. If you intend simply to refrigerate the jelly, ladle it into room temperature jars (very cold jars might crack). Let the jelly reach room temperature completely, even so far as to leave them out overnight, before putting lids on. If you wish to actually seal the jars of jelly for non-refrigerated storage, follow the instructions included with the Sure-Jell®.

STRAWBERRY JAM

In the early spring, cases or half-cases of fresh strawberries are often offered at lower prices. We would purchase a case or two on our morning run to the grocery store for a week or two, and spend much of each day washing, quartering and bagging the berries for freezing. We were generally able to stock up for an entire year this way.

Makes approximately 3-½ pints.

2 pounds strawberries (fresh or frozen; sliced or quartered)
1 cup water
1 tablespoon light corn syrup
4 cups sugar
1 package Sure-Jell® Premium Fruit Pectin - labeled "For Less or No Sugar Recipes"

Measure the sugar. In a small bowl, mix ¼ cup of the measured sugar with the contents of the Sure-Jell® packet. In a stockpot, mix the strawberries, water and corn syrup. If the strawberries are frozen, heat the mixture until they thaw. Stir the pectin/sugar into the strawberries. Bring the resulting mixture to a full rolling boil, stirring very often. Stir the remaining sugar in quickly and let the mixture reach a rolling boil once again. Boil for 1 minute and remove from heat.

Health food codes prevented us from actually sealing our jars of jam and jelly. So, they required refrigeration and had a finite shelf life. If you intend simply to refrigerate the jelly, let it sit for 15-30 minutes then ladle it into room temperature jars (very cold jars might crack). Let the jam reach room temperature completely, even so far as to leave them out overnight, before putting lids on. If you wish to actually seal the jars of jam for non-refrigerated storage, follow the instructions included with the Sure-Jell®.

Although our local fame was generally for the exotic European pastries and cakes, the lunch menu is what really kept the checkbook balance up. Uncomplicated choices of sandwiches could be combined with the soup of the day, the ever present chili or the wintertime offering of beef stew. For those with a lighter appetite, we had a small choice of green salads.

To order a sandwich required three decisions. First was the choice of breads. French, Whole Wheat or, if you felt like treating yourself, a Croissant. We did have the occasional customer that paid the nominal fee to have one of the French bread rolls sliced for a sandwich (which was actually my very personal favorite). Next was the decision about which meat to have in it, or whether to order the vegetarian. Lastly a customer had to decide which extras to pay for to make the perfect flavor combination. Cheese – Swiss, American or cheddar, sliced tomatoes, sprouts (alfalfa or clover), fresh avocado or cucumber slices marinated in our homemade Italian dressing. When the sandwich was prepared, it gained a portion of our homemade mayonnaise (lots or a little, depending on the request) and a leaf of green leaf lettuce. It was the general consensus that the mayonnaise, then the bread, were the ingredients that were truly unique to the Délice tradition.

Some of the combinations that customers came up with seemed, well, less than appetizing by our personal standards, but then again, Walter often ate a French bread roll with egg salad, tuna salad, salami and a very generous sprinkling of garlic powder.

So, what I'm trying to say is that although the sandwich recipes seem very straight forward, the reality is that there are an endless number of combinations of the simplest ingredients. For example, you can fix a ham and cheese sandwich every day of the week, but with a different cheese each day, the ham sliced thin one week, the ham sliced thick the next, sprouts one day, marinated cucumber the next. Skip the mayonnaise once in a while and substitute ranch dressing or a fine mustard.

Bon appétite.

The Lunch Menu

"Look at the old photos."

Ham and Cheese Sandwich on sliced French Bread (page 140), Chicken Noodle Soup (page 146)

Mark Hatch Photography

Beef Stew (page 150)

Mark Hatch Photography

Vegetarian Sandwich on sliced French Bread (page 144), Potato Salad (page 155), Tomato Soup (page 146)

Mark Hatch Photography

Mushroom Shell (page 153), with a tossed salad

Chicken Sandwich on sliced Whole Wheat Bread (page 141), Lentil Soup (page 148)

Mark Hatch Photography

Potato Soup with a French Bread Roll (page 147), whipped butter "flower" (page 137)

Mark Hatch Photography

Tuna Salad Sandwich on sliced French Bread (page 142), Chili Con Carne (page 149)

Mark Hatch Photography

Sausage Platter (page 155), Potato Salad (page 155)

Mark Hatch Photography

Cold Gazpacho Soup (page 148)

Roast Beef Sandwiches (page 141) on
Croissants (page 33), with prepared
horseradish

Mark Hatch Photography

Hot Swiss (page 152)

Mark Hatch Photography

Chef Salad (page 151),
Spinach Salad (page 151)

Mark Hatch Photography

Swiss Style Spaghetti (page 159)

Rösti (page 158)

Erica's Tomato Soup (page 158)

Crepes filled with
cinnamon apple slices
(page 161)

Egg Salad Sandwich on sliced Whole Wheat Bread (page 142), Vegetable Soup (page 147)

Mark Hatch Photography

Meatrolls (page 154)

Flan or Baked Custard (page 160)

Fixings

MAYONNAISE

The Mayonnaise was the special ingredient in the Egg Salad, the Tuna Salad and the Potato Salad. "Extra mayo" on a sandwich was a frequent customer request. Roughly once a week we would make the mayonnaise; enough to fill a five-gallon plastic bucket.

The likelihood that the ingredients will successfully combine is increased if the egg yolks are room temperature.

Makes one pint.

1-⅓ cups vegetable oil
2 egg yolks
heaped ¼ teaspoon salt
¼ teaspoon ground black pepper
2 teaspoons yellow mustard

Measure the oil and set it aside. Whether or not you intend to whip the oil in by hand or in a mixer, use a fork or a hand-held wire whip to mix the salt, pepper and mustard into the egg yolks. By hand or with a mixer, use a wire whip to whip the oil into the egg mixture one tablespoon at a time, being sure that each tablespoon is well incorporated before adding the next tablespoonful.

Keep refrigerated in an airtight container or canning jar for as long as a couple of weeks.

ITALIAN DRESSING

This dressing, in combination with the homemade Mayonnaise, was the secret ingredient in the Potato Salad. It was also the special marinade for the cucumber slices that went into the Vegetarian Sandwiches. We changed the proportion of vinegar to oil from the directions on the package. Grolsch and French beer bottles with the nice resealable tops are what we kept the dressing refrigerated in.

Makes 1 cup.

1 packet (7-ounce) Good Seasons Italian Salad Dressing
  & Recipe Mix®
7 tablespoons red wine vinegar*
2 tablespoons water
½ cup salad oil*

Stir together the vinegar, water and dressing mix. Add the oil and stir vigorously. Refrigerate.

*Cynthia's Note: For a more flavorful version, substitute 2 tablespoons of balsamic vinegar for 2 tablespoons of the wine vinegar. I also use olive oil for half of the salad oil.

RANCH DRESSING

The secret to our ranch dressing was the homemade Mayonnaise.

Prepare Mayonnaise (see recipe above).

1 cup mayonnaise
1 packet (.4-ounce) Hidden Valley Buttermilk Recipe
  Ranch Dressing Mix
1 cup (1 half-pint) buttermilk

In a bowl, use a wire whip to combine the cup of homemade mayonnaise, the buttermilk and the dressing mix. Refrigerate.

Délice

MARINATED CUCUMBER SLICES

Every few days we would peel and slice 3 cucumbers and pour a half of a bottle of our Italian dressing over the slices and let them marinate overnight. These were originally intended for the vegetarian sandwiches, but over time we got more requests for them on the other sandwiches. Eventually we made it official and added them to the menu as one of the optional items for the sandwiches.

Makes 2 sandwich-size portions.

Prepare the Italian dressing (page 136) a couple of hours ahead or the day before, or purchase your favorite commercial version.

1 cucumber
1-½ tablespoons of Italian dressing

Peel a section of a cucumber and slice 12 thin slices. Marinate the slices in 1-½ tablespoons of Italian dressing for several hours or overnight.

ROASTED CHICKEN

The early morning routine included setting several chickens to roasting in the ovens. Once they were done and had had time to cool, someone was elected to debone all the meat and cut it into ½ - 1 inch bits. These bits were then placed in the sandwich counter to make chicken sandwiches with. Any chicken that was left at day's end was frozen and then used the following Tuesday for the Chicken Noodle Soup.

one 5-5-½ pound fryer chicken
salt

Preheat oven to 450°.

Line a baking pan with parchment paper or aluminum foil to ease cleanup. Remove the chicken from its packaging and place it in the pan. Remove the neck and giblets from the cavity. If preparing the chicken for sandwiches, leave

the neck in the pan and debone it with the rest of the meat. If preparing the chicken for soup, retain the neck and cut both wings off. Use these parts to prepare the chicken stock for the soup while the chicken roasts or freeze them to make the stock later. Leave the remaining giblets in the pan to roast if someone will enjoy them.

Sprinkle the top of the chicken liberally with salt. Place the chicken, uncovered, into the oven. Reduce the oven temperature to 350°. Roast for 1 hour, 30 minutes.

Check for doneness by pulling the legs away. If the fluids run clear, the meat is done. If the meat around the joint is still red, place the chicken back into the oven for an additional 10 minutes.

Let the chicken rest until cool enough to handle before deboning the meat.

WHIPPED BUTTER

Whipping butter, or a combination of butter and margarine, briefly with a little bit of crushed ice creates a light, fluffy butter that spreads easily over warm bread.

Once whipped, create decorative, individual servings by using a pastry tube with a large star tip in it to pipe butter "flowers" onto a parchment lined cookie sheet.

Freeze the "flowers" until hard. Place them into an airtight container and remove them as needed. They will reach room temperature in just a few minutes. Or, if individual servings are too much, keep the whipped butter in a container in the refrigerator.

Morning chicken

Sandwiches (for two)

HAM & CHEESE SANDWICHES FOR TWO

This was the number one selling sandwich on our menu. We used Hormel's 95% lean ham and sliced it thin, then matched it with a medium priced Swiss cheese, also sliced thinly.

Bake the French or Whole Wheat bread (pages 27, 29) or Croissants (page 33) - or purchase the bread of your choice.

Prepare the Mayonnaise (page 136).

4 slices bread or 2 croissants
4 ounces thinly sliced ham
4 slices Swiss cheese (or the cheese of your choice)
2 leaves green leaf lettuce

optional: tomato slices, avocado slivers, alfalfa or clover sprouts or marinated cucumber (page 137)

If using croissants, carefully slice them through horizontally. Spread mayonnaise onto the four slices of bread or the 4 croissant halves. Divide the sliced ham between two of the bread slices or the 2 croissant bottoms. Top with the cheese and whichever optional ingredients you prefer. Finish each sandwich with a leaf of green leaf lettuce. Place the tops on and cut the sandwiches in half. Serve with bowls of hot chicken noodle soup.

TURKEY SANDWICHES FOR TWO

It was amazing how many turkey sandwiches we would sell in the days surrounding Thanksgiving. The simplest of all the sandwiches, it is important that the turkey be sliced very thinly.

Bake the French or Whole Wheat bread (pages 27, 29) or Croissants (page 33) - or purchase the bread of your choice.

Prepare the Mayonnaise (page 136).

4 slices bread or 2 croissants
4 ounces thinly sliced turkey
2 leaves green leaf lettuce

optional: cheese slices, tomato slices, avocado slivers, alfalfa or clover sprouts or marinated cucumber (page 137)

If using croissants, carefully slice them through horizontally. Spread mayonnaise onto the four slices of bread or the 4 croissant halves. Divide the sliced turkey between 2 of the bread slices or the 2 croissant bottoms. Top with the optional ingredients you prefer. Finish each sandwich with a leaf of green leaf lettuce. Place the tops on and cut the sandwiches in half. Serve with green side salads.

Délice

ROAST BEEF SANDWICHES FOR TWO

One of the first foods to go into the oven each morning was a beef rump roast. Purchased at the local grocery, it was placed fat side up into a baking pan, sprinkled with salt and left in the oven 25-30 minutes per pound. After cooling a least 10-15 minutes, the roast was placed onto the antique Hobart meat slicer and sliced across the grain.

Walter's favorite addition to this sandwich was prepared horseradish.

Bake the French or Whole Wheat bread (pages 27, 29) or Croissants (page 33) - or purchase the bread of your choice.

Prepare the Mayonnaise (page 136).

4 slices of bread or 2 croissants
4-5 ounces thinly sliced roast beef
2 leaves of green leaf lettuce

optional: cheese slices, tomato slices, avocado slivers, alfalfa or clover sprouts or marinated cucumber slices (page 137)

If using croissants, carefully slice them through horizontally. Spread the mayonnaise onto the four slices of bread or the 4 croissant halves. Divide the sliced roast beef between two of the slices. Top with the optional ingredients you prefer. Finish each sandwich with a leaf of green leaf lettuce. Place the tops on and cut in half. Serve with potato chips.

CHICKEN SANDWICHES FOR TWO

We often had to explain to new customers that the chicken sandwich was not chicken salad; it was bits of freshly roasted chicken. Roasting a couple of chickens was an integral part of our early morning routine. If roasting a whole chicken does not fit your lifestyle or timetable, purchase a rotisserie chicken from the local market.

Bake the French or Whole Wheat bread (pages 27, 29) or Croissants (page 33) - or purchase the bread of your choice.

Prepare the Mayonnaise (page 136).

Roast a chicken (see Roasted Chicken, page 137) – or purchase a rotisserie chicken.

4 slices bread or 2 croissants
1-½ cups chopped roasted chicken (mixed white and
    dark meat)
2 leaves green leaf lettuce

optional: cheese slices, tomato slices, avocado slivers, alfalfa or clover sprouts or marinated cucumber (page 137)

If using croissants, carefully slice them through horizontally. Spread mayonnaise onto the four slices of bread or the 4 croissant halves. Divide the chopped chicken between 2 of the bread slices or the 2 croissant bottoms. Top with the optional ingredients you prefer. Finish each sandwich with a leaf of green leaf lettuce. Place the tops on and cut the sandwiches in half. Serve with cups of lentil soup.

EGG SALAD SANDWICHES FOR TWO

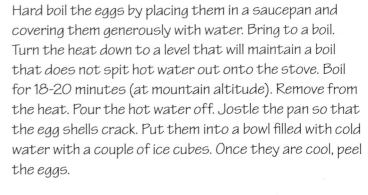

We had a number of customers that were passionate about our egg salad. The "secret" ingredient was the homemade Mayonnaise. For those individuals that have chosen the low-carb lifestyle, serve a scoop of the egg salad over a plate of lettuce greens with several slices of ripe tomato.

Bake the French or Whole Wheat bread (pages 27, 29) or Croissants (page 33) – or purchase the bread of your choice.

Prepare the Mayonnaise (page 136).

4 slices of bread or 2 croissants
4 eggs
2 teaspoons sweet pickle relish
1 tablespoon mayonnaise
2 leaves of green leaf lettuce

optional: tomato slices, cheese slices, avocado slivers, alfalfa or clover sprouts or marinated cucumber (page 137)

Hard boil the eggs by placing them in a saucepan and covering them generously with water. Bring to a boil. Turn the heat down to a level that will maintain a boil that does not spit hot water out onto the stove. Boil for 18-20 minutes (at mountain altitude). Remove from the heat. Pour the hot water off. Jostle the pan so that the egg shells crack. Put them into a bowl filled with cold water with a couple of ice cubes. Once they are cool, peel the eggs.

Cut the eggs up using a knife or egg slicer (we used a round cookie cutter). Add the sweet pickle relish and the mayonnaise. Cover with plastic. Refrigerate for an hour or up to three days.

If using croissants, carefully slice them through horizontally. Prepare two sandwiches with lettuce and your preferred combination of the optional items. Serve with cups of vegetable soup.

TUNA SALAD SANDWICHES FOR TWO

I dedicate this recipe to my best friend, fellow dog lover and hiking buddy, Linda, whose passion for tuna sandwiches (of nearly any kind) is nearly insatiable. The secret ingredient, as with any of our meat salads, was the homemade mayonnaise.

Bake the French or Whole Wheat bread (pages 27, 29) or Croissants (page 33) - or purchase the bread of your choice.

Prepare the Mayonnaise (page 136).

2 (6 ounce) cans light tuna in water
½ stick celery
2-3 tablespoons mayonnaise
2 leaves of green leaf lettuce

optional: tomato slices, cheese slices, avocado slivers, alfalfa or clover sprouts or marinated cucumber (page 137)

Drain the water from the tuna. Use a fork to scrape the tuna into a bowl. Cut the ½ celery stick in half lengthwise, then chop it into small pieces. Add the celery to the tuna. Add mayonnaise to the tuna/celery until it is your preferred consistency.

If using croissants, carefully slice them through horizontally. Spread additional mayonnaise onto the four slices of bread or the 4 croissant halves, if desired. Spoon the tuna salad onto two slices of the bread or the croissant bottoms. Add any of the optional items that appeal to you and top with lettuce. Place the tops on and cut the sandwiches in half. Serve with bowls of chili con carne.

Délice

SALAMI SANDWICHES FOR TWO

We sliced all of our lunchmeat on the premises, thereby allowing us to control just how thin the slices of meat were. Salami should be sliced paper thin – thin enough that a person can see through tiny little holes in the slices. The thin slices are then "crumpled up" onto the bread instead of laying flat and lifeless.

Bake the French or Whole Wheat bread (pages 27, 29) or Croissants (page 33) - or purchase the bread of your choice.

Prepare the Mayonnaise (page 136).

4 slices of bread or 2 croissants
4-6 ounces thinly-sliced Genoa salami
2 leaves green leaf lettuce

optional: cheese slices, tomato slices, avocado slivers, alfalfa or clover sprouts or marinated cucumber slices (page 137)

If using croissants, carefully slice them through horizontally. Spread the mayonnaise onto the four slices of bread or the 4 croissant halves. Place half of the salami on each of two of them. Top with cheese or whichever optional ingredients you prefer. Finish each sandwich with a leaf of green leaf lettuce. Place the tops on and cut in half. Serve with vegetable soup or homemade potato salad.

LIVERWURST SANDWICHES FOR TWO

Liverwurst (or braunschweiger) is a very rare item on a modern luncheon menu. It is one of those foods that people take sides about – either they really like it or they won't touch it. We had a gentleman who always requested two slices of liverwurst on his vegetarian sandwich. I always found it amusing that a number of our regular customers would only order the liverwurst if they were not accompanied by family members. Thin slices of raw red onion were a popular addition to this sandwich. The braunschweiger that we used can generally be purchased from the deli counter at the local grocery store. Ask them to slice just what you need.

Bake the French or Whole Wheat bread (pages 27, 29) or Croissants (page 33) - or purchase the bread of your choice.

Prepare the Mayonnaise (page 136).

4 slices of bread or 2 croissants
4 (¼-inch thick) slices Wilson's® braunschweiger
2 leaves of green leaf lettuce

optional: sliced yellow or red onion, tomato slices, cheese slices, avocado slivers, alfalfa or clover sprouts or marinated cucumber (page 137)

If using croissants, carefully slice them through horizontally. Spread mayonnaise onto the four slices of bread or the 4 croissant halves. Place two slices of the liverwurst onto each of the two of the bread slices. Add whichever optional items are your favorite. Place a leaf of green leaf lettuce on top of each sandwich and then add the top slice of bread. Cut each sandwich in half. Serve with bowls of hot potato soup.

VEGETARIAN SANDWICHES FOR TWO

The "vegie" sandwich was a direct descendant of sandwiches that Walter fixed for his own lunch, using all the "optional" fixings that went on the regular lunchmeat sandwiches. The secret ingredient was the cucumber slices marinated in our homemade Italian salad dressing. Customers took great liberties with this particular sandwich, adding such things as liverwurst or chicken. Use your imagination.

Bake the French or Whole Wheat bread (pages 27, 29) or Croissants (page 33) - or purchase the bread of your choice.

Prepare the Mayonnaise (page 136).

12 thin slices cucumber
1-½ tablespoons Italian dressing
4 slices bread or 2 croissants
4 slices Swiss cheese
4 slices tomato
1 ounce alfalfa or clover sprouts
½ ripe avocado
2 leaves green leaf lettuce

optional: any kind of meat

Peel a section of a cucumber and slice 12 thin slices. Marinate the slices in 1-½ tablespoons of Italian dressing (page 136) for several hours or overnight.

If using croissants, carefully slice them through horizontally. Spread the mayonnaise onto the four slices of bread or the 4 croissant halves. Onto one slice of bread or one lower half of a croissant, place 2 slices of Swiss cheese, 2 slices of tomato, half of the sprouts, 6 slices of marinated cucumber, and a leaf of green leaf lettuce. Onto the "top" bread slice or croissant, spoon or slice ¼ of a ripe avocado. Flip the slice with the avocado over onto the vegetable covered slice. Repeat the process for the second sandwich. Cut the sandwiches in half. Serve with tomato soup or potato salad.

The gingerbread Jeep, Winterskol Parade, 1961

Délice

Soups, Entrées and Sides

TOMATO SOUP

This is a very simple and very quick recipe that we served on Mondays. If you like the soup with a little more substance, add a handful of small pasta or instant rice 10 minutes before serving. Use petite cut diced tomatoes for a daintier version. Have additional pepper available for anyone who likes their soup hotter.

Makes 3 cups (2 large servings).

⅓ cup chopped yellow onion
1 tablespoon vegetable oil
1 (14.5-ounce) can diced tomatoes

1 (14.5-ounce) can of water
½ teaspoon salt
½ teaspoon garlic powder
½ teaspoon sugar
¼ teaspoon ground black pepper

In a large saucepan, sauté the chopped onion in the oil until it just begins to brown. Add the diced tomatoes and the can of water. Bring to a boil. Stir in the seasonings and simmer for 15-20 minutes. Serve with crackers or bread.

CHICKEN NOODLE SOUP

Because Tuesday was chicken noodle soup day, it was often the busiest day of the week, especially if the weather was inclement. We had many customers who we only saw on Tuesdays. I believe that the secrets to our soup were that the chicken was oven roasted, not boiled, and that we assembled each bowl of noodles, chicken and broth as it was ordered.

If taking the time to roast a chicken is not realistic for you, purchase a rotisserie chicken (original flavor) from the local market. The soup will taste a bit different, but will still be a close cousin.

Makes approximately 4 (1-⅓ cup) servings.

Oven roast a chicken (see Roasted Chicken, page 137).

3 cups water
4 ounces wide egg noodles (2 cups, dry)
1 (14-ounce) can chicken broth
1-½ teaspoons chicken bouillon granules
⅛ teaspoon ground black pepper

If you roasted a chicken:
Put the raw or roasted neck and/or the wing(s) and 3 cups of water into a stockpot or large saucepan. Bring the water to a boil, turn the heat down, cover the pan and simmer for 30 minutes. While that is boiling, remove all the meat from the chicken and cut a mixture of white and dark meat into 1 inch pieces until you have 2 cups of chunked chicken.

If you purchased a roasted chicken:
Remove all of the meat from the bones and set the meat aside. Place the bones and the water into a stockpot or large saucepan. Bring the water to a boil, turn the heat down, cover the pan and simmer for 30 minutes. While it is boiling, cut a mixture of the white and dark meat into 1 inch pieces until you have 2 cups of chunked chicken.

While the chicken parts are simmering, in a separate large saucepan, boil the egg noodles according to the directions. When done, drain them and rinse with cold water. Set them aside.

Remove the chicken parts from the simmering water and discard them. To the resulting broth, add the can of chicken broth, the bouillon and the pepper. Bring to a boil. Remove from heat.

Into soup bowls, place roughly one cup of egg noodles and a ½ cup of chicken chunks. Pour or ladle the hot chicken broth over the noodles and chicken. Serve.

Délice

VEGETABLE SOUP

Wednesday was Vegetable Soup day. We always cut the vegetables on Tuesday afternoon and kept them in a plastic bag in the refrigerator overnight, thereby making the morning's soup preparation the simplest of the week. The real dilemma was guessing how much soup to fix on any given day; the weather being a big influence. One day the local market was out of green cabbage so we used red instead. The resulting soup tasted the same, but was a most remarkable shade of purple.

Makes approximately 8 cups.

1 cup chopped green cabbage
1 cup chopped celery
1 cup chopped carrot (1 large carrot)
1 cup chopped fresh or frozen cauliflower
1 cup chopped fresh or frozen broccoli (or snap peas or
    green beans)

7 cups water
½ cup canned diced tomatoes
1 teaspoon salt
¼ teaspoon garlic powder
⅛ teaspoon ground black pepper
½ teaspoon sugar
¼ of a Knorr vegetarian bouillon cube® (optional; does
    add msg)

Chop all the vegetables and put them into a stockpot. Add the water. Cover the pot and bring the whole to a boil. Turn the heat down so that the vegetables continue at a low boil until the carrots are fork tender (approximately 30 minutes). Add the diced tomatoes and the seasonings. Simmer for 5 minutes.

POTATO SOUP

Thursday was potato soup day. Use dairy-free potato flakes and omit the beef bouillon to create a dairy-free, vegetarian soup.

Makes approximately 4 cups (4 small servings).

⅔ cup chopped onion
1 tablespoon vegetable oil
1 large russet potato (2 cups, peeled and cut in
    ½ inch pieces)
8 cups water
¼ teaspoon ground black pepper
½ teaspoon garlic powder
½ teaspoon salt
¼ teaspoon ground nutmeg
1 teaspoon parsley flakes or chopped dried chives
¼ teaspoon beef bouillon crystals (optional)
½ teaspoon yellow mustard
¾ cup instant potato flakes

Place the chopped onion and oil into a large saucepan or a stockpot. Sauté the onions in the oil over medium heat until the onions just begin to brown. Add the potato pieces and the water. Bring the water to a boil, then turn the heat down just a bit so that a good boil is maintained. Boil the potatoes until their corners become rounded (approximately 45-60 minutes). Stir in the seasonings and the mustard. Stir in the instant potato flakes and heat through. Serve with a sprinkle of parsley flakes across the top, accompanied by saltines or bread rolls.

LENTIL SOUP

Lentil soup meant that it was Friday. Unlike beans, lentils do not require hours of cooking. This meant that if we forgot to set them to soaking in cold water overnight, there was still a hope that the soup would be ready in time for lunch hour. This particular soup is especially good as "leftovers". There is something about letting it sit in the refrigerator overnight that actually enhances its flavor.

Makes approximately 4-½ cups.

1 cup dried lentils
8 cups water
½ strip of bacon
½ cup chopped onion
2 tablespoons vegetable oil
½ cup diced tomatoes
1-¾ teaspoons salt
1-½ teaspoons garlic powder
½ teaspoon ground black pepper
½ teaspoon yellow mustard

In a stockpot or large saucepan, bring the lentils in the water to a boil. Turn the heat down so that the lentils continue at a low, but not a rolling, boil. Boil for 1 hour.

Cut the bacon into small slivers. In a small saucepan, sauté them on low heat for 2 minutes. Into the same pan, add the chopped onion. Sauté the onions with the bacon until the onions begin to brown. Add the bacon and the sautéed onions to the lentils. Stir the diced tomatoes and seasonings into the lentils also. Bring the soup back to a boil for several minutes. Serve hot with crackers or bread rolls.

COLD GAZPACHO SOUP

An adaptation of a Latin dish, we only offered this soup during the hot months of summer. A Tabasco® bottle or a container of cayenne pepper were available for those customers who liked it even hotter.

Makes approximately 3 cups (2 large servings).

1 (11.5-ounce) V-8®
1 (11.5-ounce) tomato juice
¼ + ⅛ teaspoon ground black pepper
¼ + ⅛ teaspoon garlic powder
dash of Tabasco®
dash of Maggi Seasoning® (optional, contains msg)
¼ cup finely chopped green pepper
2 tablespoons chopped green onion
1 cup peeled, finely chopped cucumber

Mix the first six ingredients and chill several hours or overnight.

Peel the cucumber. Chop it and the green pepper and green onion into very small pieces. Toss them together and refrigerate.

If the soup is to be enjoyed right away mix the vegetables into the broth and serve. If prepared ahead of time or there is any likelihood of leftovers, put ½ of the chopped vegetables into a bowl and cover with ½ of the broth. The chopped vegetables can be kept in a refrigerator container (separate from the broth) for several days.

Délice

CHILI CON CARNE

The chili was one of our most consistently popular menu items. Not as spicy as many traditional versions, we had either Tabasco® or ground red pepper available for those with a taste for fire. Prepare the spice mix ahead and keep it in an airtight container for whenever the whim hits.

Makes ½ cup spice mix (enough for 4 batches of chili).

Makes approximately 7-½ cups chili.

Spice Mix:
2 tablespoons light chili powder
2 teaspoons ground black pepper
4 teaspoons salt
¼ cup granulated sugar

Chili:
½ pound ground beef (80% lean)
1 large onion, chopped (2 cups)
4-½ cups (28 + 14.5 ounces) diced tomatoes
1 (15.25-ounce) can dark red kidney beans
2 tablespoons spice mix

In a stockpot, sauté the onion and ground beef together over medium heat until the beef browns and begins to stick to the bottom of the pan. Add the diced tomatoes, kidney beans and spice mix. Bring the whole to a boil. Turn the heat down to simmer for at least 10 or 15 minutes. If you have the time, simmering it longer is even better. Serve with French bread rolls, crackers or corn chips.

Leftovers can be refrigerated for several days or frozen, but should be brought to a boil before serving again.

"If the soup is vegetable, it must be Wednesday."

BEEF STEW

For many years, Mr. Gerbaz hinted to us that we needed to offer beef stew in the wintertime. Eventually Walter studied many different recipes and put together his version of beef stew. His twist: red wine (Chianti to be exact). To make the recipe easier to work with on our schedule, we would often brown and then boil the meat the day before, let the whole thing cool to room temperature and refrigerate it overnight. The next morning, all we needed to do was reheat the meat still in the water, boil the potatoes, carrots and onions and assemble it all.

Makes approximately 7 cups (4 large servings).

1-¼ pounds beef stew meat
1 tablespoon vegetable oil
8 cups water, divided
1 bay leaf
2 large Russet potatoes
½ pound (2 cups) baby carrots
¼ pound (1 cup) frozen pearl onions
¾ cup frozen peas
¼ teaspoon ground black pepper
⅛ teaspoon ground clove
¾ teaspoon garlic powder
2 teaspoons salt
1-½ teaspoons sugar
1 teaspoon yellow mustard
3 tablespoons Chianti (or other red wine)
4 tablespoons corn starch
4 tablespoons cold water

In a stockpot, brown the stew meat in the vegetable oil over medium heat until the pieces have browned on all sides. Add 5 cups of water and the bay leaf. Bring to a boil. Turn the heat down, cover the pan and simmer for a total of 2-¼ hours. While the meat is boiling, peel the potatoes and cut them into 1 inch chunks. Place them into a container and cover them completely with cold water. Set them aside or even refrigerate.

Once the meat has boiled for 1-½ hours, check it and, if necessary, add ½ cup of hot water to keep the meat covered. Let it continue to simmer. Drain the water from the potato chunks. Place the potato chunks and the carrots into a large saucepan or stockpot with 3 cups of water. Bring them to a boil. Turn the heat down, cover the pan and keep at a low boil for 20 minutes. Add the pearl onions to the carrots and potatoes. Bring the pot back to a boil, then allow it to simmer until the carrots are fork tender (another 20-25 minutes). Remove from heat.

Once the meat is easily chewable, remove and discard the bay leaf. Drain 1 cup of water off of the cooked carrots, potatoes, and pearl onions and discard it. Add the carrots, potatoes and pearl onions with the remaining water to the stew meat. Also add the peas, the seasonings, the mustard and the red wine. Bring the whole to a boil. Mix the cornstarch into the cold water. Stir the cornstarch mixture into the stockpot. Heat briefly, but do not bring to a full boil. Remove from heat. Serve with bread rolls, crackers or sandwiches.

Délice

CHEF'S SALAD

This menu item was actually listed as a Small Chef's Salad, but the majority of our customers felt that the "small" was a misnomer. It covered an entire platter. We initially used iceberg lettuce, but as the health benefits of greener lettuce became known, we switched to green leaf lettuce. Use the lettuce of your choice, or mix lettuce with fresh spinach.

Makes 1 chef's salad.

Bake French or Whole Wheat bread rolls (page 27 or 29) or purchase the bread roll of your choice.

Prepare Italian Dressing (page 136), or Ranch Dressing (page 136) or purchase the dressing of your choice.

4-5 ounces lettuce
1 hard boiled egg
4 slices tomato
2 slices Swiss cheese
2 slices ham
3-4 ounces salad dressing of choice

Wash the lettuce. Cut or tear the lettuce into bite-size pieces and place onto a full-size plate. Slice the hard boiled egg. Place the slices along one edge of the salad. Place the tomato slices along the opposite edge. Place the two slices of Swiss cheese onto a cutting board so that they overlap. Place the ham slices onto the cheese. Roll the ham up in the cheese. Cut the rolled ham and cheese and place it across the top of the salad. Serve the salad with a bread roll, butter and salad dressing.

SPINACH SALAD

A Spinach Salad was a meal. We covered an entire platter with fresh spinach, dressed it up, placed a 3 ounce paper cup of salad dressing at one end of the platter and served it up with a fresh bread roll and whipped butter. Simplify by purchasing packaged salad spinach and getting a hard boiled egg from the deli.

Makes 1 spinach salad.

Bake French or Whole Wheat bread rolls (page 27 or 29) or purchase the bread roll of your choice.

Prepare Italian Dressing (page 136), or Ranch Dressing (page 136) or purchase the dressing of your choice.

3 ounces fresh spinach
1 hard boiled egg
4 slices tomato
1 large mushroom
1-2 teaspoons bacon bits
3-4 ounces salad dressing of choice

Wash and de-stem the spinach. Place onto full-size plate. Slice the hard boiled egg. Place the slices along one edge of the salad. Place the tomato slices along the opposite edge. Cut the mushroom into thin slices and scatter across the top of the salad. Sprinkle the bacon bits across the top of the mushroom. Serve the salad with a bread roll, butter and salad dressing.

HOT SWISS FOR TWO

To quote the menu, the Hot Swiss was a "hot open-faced ham, cheese and tomato sandwich with a touch of wine". The expression "Hot Swiss" was used because Swiss cheese was used, but Walter often used the expression to refer to himself, frequently disconcerting an unsuspecting customer.

Prepare and bake the French Bread (page 27) or purchase a similar bread.

4 slices French (or Italian style) bread
16 slices tomato
3 ounces thinly-sliced ham
4 slices Swiss cheese
1/3 cup shredded Mozzarella cheese
2 tablespoons Chablis (or any white wine)

Preheat oven to 400°.

Cut the bottom crust away from two of the bread slices. Place these two slices onto a metal baking sheet. Place the remaining two slices of bread flat or "open" with the bottom crust of each slice butted up against the crustless bottom of one of the first two slices. Place four slices of tomato on top of each pair of bread slices. Divide the ham between the two "sandwiches". Place another four tomato slices over the ham on each "sandwich". Cover the tomato slices with two slices of the Swiss cheese. Top each "sandwich" with half of the shredded Mozzarella cheese.

Place the baking sheet into the oven for 15-18 minutes or until the cheese melts and begins to brown. Remove from the oven and place the "sandwiches" on plates. Drizzle 1 tablespoon of Chablis or other white wine over each "sandwich". Serve hot with lentil soup or a tossed salad.

Délice

MUSHROOM PUFFPASTRY SHELLS

We kept this mushroom sauce in a small crockpot on low heat. The frozen puffpastry shells were heated in the oven as needed. Each shell was filled just to overflowing. Simple, but very tasty. If puffpastry shells are not an option, serve the sauce over rice. Prefer not to spend time in food prep? Purchase the mushrooms already sliced.

Makes 8 small sauce-filled pastry shells.

Prepare puffpastry (page 48) the day before or several hours ahead (or purchase puffpastry shells from the freezer section at the grocery store.)

If using homemade puffpastry, prepare an eggwash (see Glossary) and set it aside.

1 pound mushrooms
3 tablespoons butter
2-½ cups warm water
1 Knorr vegetable bouillon cube® (or 2 teaspoons beef bouillon granules)
¼ teaspoon Morton's Nature's Seasons®
pinch of salt
¼ cup (2 fluid ounces) white wine (We used Chablis)
¼ cup cornstarch
½ cup cold water

The puffpastry shells:
Preheat oven all the way to 400°.

If using purchased puffpastry shells, prepare them according to package directions. If using homemade puffpastry, line a baking sheet with parchment. Cut the puffpastry in half. (Freeze other half for later use.) On a lightly floured surface, roll the puffpastry out until it is ¼ inch thick. Use a large round cutter to cut circles or a jagger (see Glossary) or knife to cut squares or triangles out of the dough. Place the resulting pieces onto the baking sheet. Lightly brush the top surface of the dough with eggwash, being careful not to let it run down the sides. With a small knife, carefully cut only into the top portion of the dough to create a line roughly ½ inch from the edge. (After baking, this center piece will become a lid.)

Bake for 20-25 minutes or until the top of each piece is lightly brown. Use a small knife to gently cut the "lid" out of each piece and perhaps remove a bit of the interior dough.

The mushroom sauce:
In a small bowl, mix the cornstarch and the cold water. Set it aside. If the mushrooms are not already sliced, wash them or wipe them off with a damp towel. Slice them thinly. In a stockpot, sauté the sliced mushrooms in the butter over medium heat for 7-10 minutes or just until the mushrooms begin to soften and cook down. Add the warm water, the bouillon cube and the seasonings. Bring the mixture just to a boil. Turn the heat down to a simmer. Stir the wine in. Restir the cornstarch/cold water mixture and stir it into the mushroom sauce. Heat the mushroom sauce just to below a boil. Remove from heat.

Place a pastry shell onto a serving plate, lift its "lid", ladle ½ cup of the mushroom sauce into it and place the lid on top of the sauce. Repeat for each shell. Serve with potato salad or a green side salad.

MEATROLLS

Meatrolls can be made ahead of time and frozen in the unbaked state or baked and then frozen for several weeks. Serve baked Meatrolls with soup or salad for a tasty hot meal, or serve them cold as a fun picnic food or lunchbox treat. Cut them into small pieces as hor d'oevres and dip them in your favorite barbeque sauce.

Makes 8 meatrolls.

Prepare puffpastry (page 48) the day before or several hours ahead (or purchase it from the freezer section at the grocery store.)

Prepare an eggwash (see Glossary).

1-½ cups chopped yellow onion
2 tablespoons vegetable oil
1 pound ground beef (80% lean)
3 sticks chopped celery
2-½ cups chopped cabbage
½ teaspoon salt
½ teaspoon beef bouillon crystals
½ teaspoon garlic powder
½ teaspoon yellow mustard
⅛ teaspoon ground black pepper

Sauté the onions in the oil over medium heat until they become lightly browned. Meanwhile, put the chopped celery and cabbage into a stockpot and cover them with cold water. Bring them to a boil. Remove from heat and drain the water off. Let them cool to room temperature (if you are in a hurry, spread them out on a tray). Combine the sautéed onions, boiled celery and cabbage, the ground beef and the seasonings. Do not overmix.

Lightly flour a rolling surface. If using purchased puffpastry sheets: gently roll each square so that it is roughly 10 x 10 inches. Cut each one in half. If using homemade puffpastry: roll the puffpastry out into a rectangle roughly 14 x 20 inches. Cut the rectangle lengthwise.

Using a pastry tube, a ziploc bag with an inch cut from one corner or your fingers, create "sausages" of all of the meat mixture along the long edges of the puffpastry rectangles. **(A)** On the opposite long edges, use a pastry brush or your fingers to apply a half inch wide strip of eggwash. For each rectangle, roll the "sausage" edge over, tucking the mixture in as you go, until the eggwashed edge is on the bottom. **(B)** Gently press the rolls flat and eggwash the tops. Cut into 6-8 inch sections. Use a small knife to cut 2-3 small slashes in each section.

To freeze:
Place the meatrolls onto a parchment lined tray or sheet. Freeze them uncovered until hard. Once hard, they can be kept in a plastic bag.

To bake:
Preheat oven all the way to 400°.

Place freshly rolled or frozen meatrolls onto an unlined baking pan with a rim. Bake for 25-40 minutes, or until the puffpastry is lightly browned.

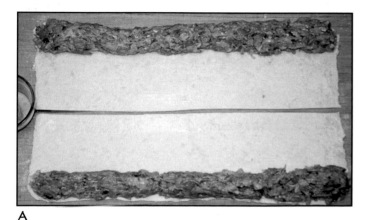

A

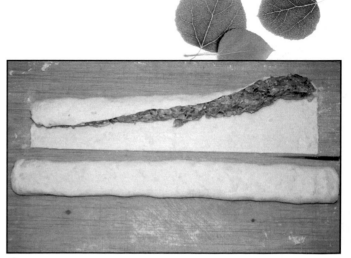

B

Délice

SAUERKRAUT (SAUSAGE PLATTER)

The Swiss Sausage Platter offered two Emmentaler sausages from Continental Sausage in Denver (use your choice of sausage), a generous portion of our potato salad, a fresh bread roll served with butter that we had whipped ourselves and a side of Walter's sauerkraut. We prepared the sauerkraut in batches large enough to fill a full-size commercial tray. We then cut the sauerkraut into small squares and froze them. Once frozen, the squares would just break apart. Heating one portion in a small saucepan only took a few minutes.

Makes approximately 2 cups (2 servings).

1 (14-ounce) can sauerkraut
½ slice bacon
2 tablespoons chopped onion
¼ teaspoon salt
⅛ teaspoon garlic powder
⅛ teaspoon ground black pepper

Pour the sauerkraut into a bowl, cover with cold water and set it aside. Slice the bacon into small pieces and cook in a large saucepan over medium heat for 2 minutes. Add the chopped onion and sauté for another 5 minutes or until the onion begins to brown. Drain the water off of the sauerkraut, but do not press all the liquid off. Add the sauerkraut to the saucepan. Stir in the remaining seasonings and heat over medium heat just until the liquid is cooked off. Serve hot.

POTATO SALAD

The potato salad was truly made from scratch; homemade Italian Dressing gave it its zing, homemade Mayonnaise made it unique. In a pinch, you can substitute purchased versions of Italian dressing and mayonnaise and still get potato salad that is better than what comes in a container.

Makes approximately 5 cups.

Prepare the Italian Dressing (page 136) a couple of hours ahead or the day before.

Prepare Mayonnaise (page 136).

3 large baker potatoes (Russett)
¼ cup chopped red onion
½ cup Italian dressing
6-8 tablespoons mayonnaise

Cut the potatoes in half lengthwise. Boil them, covered with water, until a knife will easily cut into the middle of one of them (45-60 minutes at mountain altitude). Drain and let cool to room temperature.

Peel the potatoes and cut into bite-size pieces. Mix the chopped onion and the Italian dressing into the cubed potatoes. Mix the mayonnaise in until the salad is the consistency that you prefer. Refrigerate for a couple of hours. Serve on a bed of lettuce.

View from the Glenwood store, late 1980's

Délice

Recipes from Home

As with most families, food is generally at the center of any get-together. Many of our family recipes are strongly influenced by Walter's European upbringing. Flavors that are not common "over here", we have become particularly fond of. To include a few of these foods in this book forced me to standardize several recipes that Walter would, in reality, throw together as supplies allowed. A small taste of our family's favorites.

ERICA'S TOMATO SOUP

Inspired by a Disney movie, Erica dictated this recipe to her mom before she had even learned to write.

Serves 4.

1 tablespoon olive oil
½ medium sized onion, diced
1 stick celery, diced
4 medium sized red tomatoes, diced
2 medium sized yellow tomatoes, diced
6 cups chicken broth
2 shakes pepper
½ teaspoon dried basil

Heat olive oil in a pot. Add onion and celery. Sauté until soft and onions lightly browned. Add tomatoes and chicken broth. Add pepper and basil. Stir. Bring to a boil. Then lower heat and simmer 10 minutes.

RÖSTI

Customers would often ask Walter what his favorite food was. His comeback was "a steak and a good beer", neither of which was on the menu. On the weekends though, steak and rösti were nearly inseparable at his house. Rösti is grated potatoes, stirred with sautéed onions, garlic, bacon and seasonings and allowed to brown in a pan; a European version of hash browns.

If you purchase bacon already cooked, sauté the onions in a tablespoon of olive oil.

Serves 2-4 people.

2 large Russett potatoes (4 cups grated)
1 slice bacon
1 cup chopped onion
1 tablespoon olive oil (optional)
1-2 cloves garlic (or add 1 teaspoon garlic powder with other seasonings)
½ teaspoon ground black pepper
½ teaspoon salt

Chop the onion, mince the garlic (if using clove garlic) and cut the slice of bacon into small bits. Grate the potatoes and place into a large bowl. In a large skillet, cook the bits of bacon until crispy. Spoon the bacon bits into the bowl with the grated potato, leaving the fat in the pan. Sauté the onions and garlic in the fat until they begin to brown. Add them to the grated potato. Add the seasonings to the potatoes. Stir everything into the potatoes. Place the potato mixture into the skillet on low heat. Cover the pan and allow the potatoes to cook for 10-15 minutes or until they are well browned underneath. If you are skilled in the kitchen, flip the potato "patty" over. If you are more cautious, cut the patty in half and use a spatula to turn each half over. Cover the pan and let the potatoes cook for another 10-15 minutes or until brown underneath.

Délice

SWISS STYLE SPAGHETTI

Besides steak and rösti, this is the meal that is served at informal Huber gatherings. We used to have to order Gruyère cheese from a Swiss specialty warehouse in Denver called Continental Sausage, but, now it is available in most deli cheese cases. If you don't have both kinds of cheese, you can substitute Mozzarella for part of it, but don't replace all of it. The Swiss cheese, and especially the Gruyère, are what give this dish a unique flavor. Serve with garlic bread.

Serves 2 adults.

8 ounces spaghetti, uncooked
½ cup chopped onion
1-2 cloves minced garlic (OR add 1 teaspoon garlic powder with seasonings)
1 tablespoon olive oil
2 cups chopped fresh tomato (2 large tomatoes)
¼ teaspoon salt
¼ teaspoon ground black pepper
½ teaspoon Morton's Nature Seasons®
½ teaspoon sugar
¼ cup shredded or chopped Gruyère cheese
¾ cup shredded or chopped Swiss cheese

Prepare and drain the spaghetti according to package directions.

In a stockpot, sauté the chopped onions and minced clove garlic in the olive oil over medium heat, until the onion is lightly browned. Add the chopped tomato and the seasonings. Cook over medium heat for 3-5 minutes. Turn the heat down to low. Stir the cooked spaghetti into the tomato mixture. Add the cheeses. Heat, stirring occasionally, until cheese melts. Serve.

Viola, Grandma Kinne and Walter on the deck above the second Aspen store

FLAN OR BAKED CUSTARD

Individual servings of this caramel custard were served at the larger original location in Aspen, but never at the later Glenwood Springs store. Much to my delight, this became a staple at the New Castle house after the business closed and was kept on hand in a small refrigerator. What a treat!

Makes 7 (¾-cup) servings.

1-1/6 cups sugar, divided
6 eggs
1 quart (4 cups) milk
1 teaspoon vanilla

Preheat oven to 350°.

Place 7 to 9 oven-proof ramequins into a pan (or pans) that is (are) deep enough to hold 1 inch of water. Set them aside.

Measure ½ cup of the sugar. Warm a heavy saucepan over low heat. Sprinkle a tablespoon of the sugar over the bottom of the warm pan and wait patiently until the sugar begins to melt. Resist the temptation to turn the heat up. Once the sugar in the pan begins to liquify, you may stir it with a wooden spoon. Sprinkle another spoonful of the sugar into the pan and melt it. Continue to add the sugar to the pan a spoonful at a time, stirring occasionally, until it is all melted. Divide the resulting caramel between the ramequins. Set them aside. The caramel will harden quickly. An alternative is to let the caramel harden in the pan, break it up into pieces and put the pieces into the bottoms of the ramequins.

Open and beat the eggs. Set them aside. Pour the milk and ⅔ cup of the sugar into a saucepan. Heat and stir the milk/sugar mixture over low heat just long enough for it to reach lukewarm. DO NOT let it boil. Remove the saucepan from the heat. Stir into the saucepan the beaten eggs and the vanilla. Pour or ladle the mixture through a wire strainer into the ramequins.

Place the pan with the filled ramequins into the oven. Carefully pour hot water into the pan (or pans) until it is an inch or so deep. Bake for 1 hour with the oven door held open slightly by a wooden spoon. Add water, if needed. Turn the oven temperature down 25° if the water should begin to boil. After an hour, turn the oven off, close the oven door and leave the custard in the oven for an additional hour. Be extra careful when lifting the pans from the oven, as the hot water may splash or spill.

Remove the ramequins from the water and let the custard cool briefly. To serve, run a knife between the custard and the inside edge of the ramequin. Place a small serving plate over the top of the ramequin. Very quickly invert the ramequin and plate together. Gently shake the custard out of the ramequin. The liquid caramel will run over the top of the custard. Serve warm.

Délice

CREPES

Crepes are a traditional French dessert. Cinnamon fried apples is the filling that is included here, but freshly sliced peaches with Custard Cream (page 43) or fresh strawberries with sweet whipped cream are delicious alternatives. Sprinkle powdered sugar over the top for a classy look.

Makes 7 (6 inch) apple filled crepes.

½ cup cake flour
2 tablespoons sugar
½ teaspoon salt
1 tablespoon vegetable oil
½ cup cold water
1 egg

the apple filling:
4 small granny smith apples (4 cups peeled and sliced)
3 tablespoons butter
½ cup brown sugar
2 tablespoons granulated sugar
1-½ teaspoons ground cinnamon

The apple filling:

Peel and slice each apple into 16 slices. In a large frying pan or stockpot, melt the butter over medium heat. Add the apple slices, the brown sugar, the sugar and the cinnamon. Stirring occasionally, cook for approximately 15 minutes or until the apples are fork tender. Keep warm until crepes are ready to fill.

The crepes:

In a bowl, use a wire whip to mix together the flour, the sugar and the salt. Mix in the oil and the water. Add the egg and beat it in only as long as necessary to incorporate it. Run the batter through a wire strainer into another bowl.

Heat a crepe pan or small (7 inch) teflon frying pan over medium heat. Pour just enough of the batter into the hot pan to coat the bottom of the pan, using a slanting, circular motion. Return the pan to the heat and right away loosen the edge of the crepe using a spoon or spatula. As soon as the edge begins to brown, lift the crepe and turn it over. Leave in the pan only long enough for it to lightly brown in spots. Leaving it in the pan too long will cause it to dry out. Keep crepes covered and warm until ready to fill.

Place 8 or 9 slices of the apple filling onto a crepe. For the adults, an option is to dribble Kirschwasser (Cherry Brandy) or Rum over the apple filling. Roll the apple slices up in the crepe. Sprinkle with powdered sugar or top with sweetened whip cream. Serve warm.

The "Délice", a French expression for something delicious, got its start as a Swiss Pastry Shop in 1957 in the picturesque town of Aspen, when Walter Huber, a pastry chef from Switzerland, decided to make his living there. Americans still talk romantically about the old shop on Hyman Street.

Then in Glenwood Springs, the Huber family continued the tradition of undiluted quality, where those delicious pastries were still made from scratch with nothing artificial ever added.

And of course, there was that wonderful, fresh-baked French Bread. Now those recipes are yours to take home.

Delice Cookbook
P.O. Box 5544
Eagle, CO 81631
delicerecipes@centurytel.net
(970)524-7981